Studying For Your
Social Work Degree

Transforming Social Work Practice – titles in the series

To order, please contact our distributor: BEBC Distribution, Albion Close, Parkstone, Poole, BH12 3LL. Telephone: 0845 230 9000, email: **learningmatters@bebc.co.uk**. You can also find more information on each of these titles and our other learning resources at www.learningmatters.co.uk.

Studying For Your Social Work Degree

HILARY WALKER

Series Editors: Jonathan Parker and Greta Bradley

LearningMatters

First published in 2008 by Learning Matters Ltd

British Library Cataloguing in Publication Data
A CIP record for this book is available from the British Library.

ISBN 978 1 84445 174 6

Cover design and text design by Code 5 Design Associates Ltd
Project management by Deer Park Productions, Tavistock, Devon
Typeset by Pantek Arts Ltd, Maidstone, Kent
Printed and bound in Great Britain by Bell & Bain Ltd, Glasgow

Learning Matters Ltd
33 Southernhay East
Exeter EX1 1NX
Tel: 01392 215560
info@learningmatters.co.uk
www.learningmatters.co.uk

Contents

Part Three

Acknowledgements

I would like to thank the following.

- Ruskin College, Oxford for encouraging me to take the term's study leave which gave me the opportunity to focus on working on this book.

- The editorial team at Learning Matters for their support and guidance.

- Colleagues and ex-students who so generously gave their time to reading a first draft and providing really helpful feedback.

- Friends who have supported and encouraged me.

My huge appreciation goes to all those social work students with whom I have worked – without you this book would not have been inspired or written.

So the book is particularly dedicated to the Ruskin College BA Social Work classes of 2004, in Oxford and in Suffolk, from whom I have learnt so much.

Introduction

This book is written for students undertaking an undergraduate degree in social work. Its main purpose is to support you in your studies by identifying the academic skills which must be demonstrated in an undergraduate degree and explaining how this relates to learning to become a social worker.

In 2003, a bachelor's degree with honours was introduced as the minimum qualification for all new qualifying social workers. Prior to this the qualification was a Diploma in Higher Education – equivalent to the first two years of an undergraduate degree. Requiring social work students to qualify with bachelor's degrees was in recognition of the higher-level academic skills social workers need to use when thinking about and planning their practice. It also brought the United Kingdom into line with Europe and the USA.

Most people reading this will have been selected for a place on a social work degree course or already be studying. When you examine the course programme ahead of you in more detail you will find that it has been developed and organised in order to meet general requirements laid down by the Quality Assurance Agency for Higher Education (QAA), the body with responsibility for assuring the quality of higher education courses in universities and colleges.

Each course will be organised in a different way but all courses must ensure that students studying on bachelor's degrees with honours, by the end of the programme, will have achieved what is laid down by the QAA. Because learning happens in stages, each building on earlier understanding, these requirements are organised in three levels. For full-time students these will be equivalent to the three years of the degree. For part-time students this will depend on the course. The three levels are:

Certificate (C) – the first level
Intermediate (I) – the second level
Honours (H) – the third level

Requirements at each level specify what students must be able to do and demonstrate academically at each level of the programme. All bachelor's degrees with honours must provide the opportunity for students to achieve this through teaching, learning and assessment. Of course a degree in chemistry or French will look different from a degree in social work, but the same broad academic requirements must be met.

In addition to these general requirements set by the QAA, undergraduate degrees in social work must also meet requirements laid down in the following documents.

- The National Occupational Standards for Social Work (TOPSS, 2002a): these set out both what a social worker entering employment should be able to do and what they should know.

- The Department of Health Requirements for Social Work (DoH, 2002): these were devised by this government department when the social work qualification changed from a diploma to a degree and set out some broad expectations.

- The QAA Subject Benchmark for Social Work (2008): this outlines the particular requirements for a bachelor's degree in the subject of social work; specifically what is expected of social workers awarded a degree in social work.

You will see then that achieving a degree in social work involves two main aspects. It is both about being able to practise social work and being able to demonstrate academic capabilities and skills at undergraduate degree level. A degree in social work is both a licence to practise as a professional social worker and an academic qualification. Social work is an applied academic subject so practise is an essential and core element of learning and you will be required to spend at least 200 days undertaking learning on placement in social work agencies. By the end of the course you must have met both the academic and practice standards and you will find that these two aspects are consistently and constantly interconnected. You will be required to make links between what you learn in college and the world of social work, and think about, understand, critically analyse and reflect on your practice while in placement using academic learning.

However, these requirements indicate what you must be able to do by the end of your course rather than the stages along the way. In contrast, as discussed above, the general requirements for an undergraduate honours degree set out what students should achieve at each level. Because learning is cumulative, you need to have a sound grasp of lower-level academic skills in order to build towards the higher ones. I have noticed that students can struggle later in their studies if they have not thoroughly developed foundation skills.

This book therefore takes a staged approach and is organised in three parts – each one relating to a different academic level. Hence chapters in Part One will be concerned with skills from C level, those in Part Two with skills from I level and those in Part Three with skills from H level. In each part of the book the key academic requirements at that level are explored. Every chapter indicates the specific requirements and units of competence to which it relates. On your course, in college and on placement, this division will not be as clear. However, separating them out should help you to appreciate the skills you are using and enhancing. The four chapters in Part One cover the basic, foundation academic skills. The first explores beginning your degree course and the particular characteristics of studying for social work, before discussing different approaches to learning. In Chapter 2 we focus on the underlying principles and concepts in social work with particular emphasis on the values of social work. Next, in Chapter 3 the relationship between theory and social work practice is considered, while in Chapter 4 the ingredients of academic writing are covered.

This theme is developed in Part Two, Chapter 5, which looks at more complex skills of critical analysis and understanding. Chapter 6 focuses on practice learning and how you make connections between your college studies and your experiences and practice on placement. In Chapter 7 we explore what is meant by the reflective social work practitioner and ways in which this approach can be enhanced. The final chapter of Part Two is the first of two looking at research. At this level the focus is on understanding and using research.

Part Three begins with the second research chapter, which explains how research can be subject to critical evaluation. Next, in Chapter 10, we return to thinking about learning and focus on becoming an autonomous learner. The final two chapters both consider the complexity of social work. In Chapter 11 the complicated and contradictory nature of practice is analysed and the thinking and reflective skills and strategies for social work working in this context are discussed. Finally, in Chapter 12 we consider the academic purposes of the dissertation or project and some helpful ways of approaching this important and complex piece of work.

Each chapter could be read on its own; however, you will probably find it most helpful to use all the book. This is firstly because we follow the learning journeys of three social work students throughout the book and secondly because interconnections are made between chapters. In many chapters you will find guidance on how to approach a particular academic skill. This is based on observations from my own experience as a social work tutor, what I have learnt from students and on research studies into what helps students learn. In each chapter you will find examples and activities to support you with the development of the relevant skills. However, the book is not a substitute for fully participating in all the learning activities on your course. Rather its purpose is to be complementary to your college learning and to help you make the most of them. You should always make sure you are clear about the assessment requirements and regulations on your particular programme.

Like many social work practitioners and writers, I have not yet found a term to use when referring to those members of the public with whom social workers work. None of the expressions currently used seems to appropriately convey the nature of the relationship. Hence you will find the terms 'client', 'service user' and 'people who use services' in this book – none of which is entirely satisfactory but is usable until a better alternative is found.

During my time as a tutor in social work I have come across a wide range of students. At Ruskin College nearly all students find some aspect of their academic work a challenge – sometimes because their interest is more on doing social work. One reason for writing the book was to make clear that social work cannot be practised well without good, clear, analytic thinking. Another was to provide students with some materials which would better enable them to face and overcome the challenges. I hope it has succeeded. Good luck in your studies.

Part One

Chapter 1

Beginning your social work education and training

Introduction

The purpose of this chapter is to help you to think about some important aspects of the degree in social work and what you will need to consider when embarking on your studies. It will identify what a social work degree encompasses and provide you with some ways of approaching the challenge in a positive and constructive way.

After reading this chapter you should be able to:

* understand what will be expected of you when studying for the degree in social work;

* appreciate the particular characteristics of social work education;

- identify what knowledge, skills and experience you bring to the course;

- discover some effective ways for you to study, learn and develop.

The degree in social work

As discussed in the Introduction, studying for any undergraduate degree is a demanding undertaking. For students studying for the degree in social work there are particular features and requirements which provide added challenges. In the first part of this chapter we will explore these and highlight the implications for students.

The degree in social work provides a generic qualification; you will need to develop a broad overview understanding of social work

The qualification you receive at the end of your training enables you to practise across different settings (fieldwork, residential, day care, community) and with all service user groups. In practice however, social work is now usually specialised – a social worker may be working in services for children and families and within that have a specialisation in child protection or fostering. Further, increasingly social workers are working in multi-disciplinary teams consisting of a number of other professionals. During your practice placements you will develop greater knowledge, skills and understanding in at least two different settings and with different service user groups. Once you have qualified you should have the opportunity to achieve a specialist post-qualifying award in the area of social work you have chosen. However, when studying for the degree you will need to think broadly about the very wide range of services, agencies, settings and service users which make up contemporary social work. The examples in this book have been drawn from different contexts to assist with this.

Incorporating the perspectives of people who use the services of social workers

Warren (2007, p2) notes that the *participation and involvement of service users and carers has become a key issue in current social work policy, practice, research and education*. People who use social services and carers may be involved in the selection of students, teaching and assessment on your course. When studying on a social work degree, thinking deeply about and actively taking into consideration the experiences and perspectives of people who use services and those of carers are an essential requirement (Department of Health, 2002). This means that you will have to give careful attention to the various ways of expanding your understanding of these perspectives.

There are several ways in which you can learn more about the views of service users. Firstly, you can read the *Statement of Expectations* (TOPSS, 2002b) – a document put together by a focus group of service users and carers when the degree was being developed. This states with great clarity what people who use services and carers value from social workers, and can provide a challenge to the thinking and practice of student social workers. Secondly, it is of course expected that student social workers will listen actively to the people with whom they are working on placement, in order to learn more about their lives and experiences. Thirdly, there is a growing literature which presents research into the views and voices of people who use services and carers (for example: Harding and Beresford, 1996; Twigg, 2000; Bell and Wilson, 2006; DfES, 2006a; Rose, 2006; Cree and Davis, 2007)

Sometimes students seem to find it difficult to bring this understanding of people's experiences, thoughts and feelings into their academic essays and assignments. This is one of the challenges of the degree in social work – to be able to integrate, or blend, academic ideas and personal perspectives. However, it is essential as it is part of learning to practise social work in a way that is respectful to the lives of people who use services and carers. This will be a theme throughout the book.

Social work is a profession based on a set of ethical values

From its beginnings social work has paid close attention to its values – or what is regarded as important or valuable. It has been understood that the decisions and actions of social workers, and how they go about their work, can have potential for benefit or for harm. All student social workers must learn about and be able to demonstrate these values. They must register with the General Social Care Council (GSCC) and be bound by its code of practice, which contains a set of ethical principles (GSCC, 2002). So, from the beginning of your studies you will be learning how abstract concepts, such as values and ethical principles, are relevant to practice. This will be discussed further in Chapter 2.

In order to set the scene for your studies, I have introduced the degree in social work, explored some important aspects and highlighted some of its complexities. With this in mind, in the rest of the chapter we will consider some helpful ways of getting down to studying.

Studying for your degree in social work

About you

Some of you may bring to your course a great deal of experience of life and work together with previous knowledge and useful, relevant skills – so you have plenty to build on and lots to contribute to other people's learning. However, there may be aspects of studying with which you are not familiar. Others might have some recent experience of studying but limited experience of social work issues. The following activity is designed to help you to become more self aware of what you bring with you to the course.

ACTIVITY 1.1

What I bring to my degree in social work

Try to take a step back and think about yourself, and answer the questions set out below.

- *What experience, knowledge and skills do you bring to the course?*

- *What aspects of the course do you feel fairly comfortable about tackling?*

- *What aspects of the course might be a real challenge for you?*

Record your answers to these questions and note the date.

CASE STUDY

Answers from three students

Nicola Wilson (37 years) wrote as follows.

- *I feel rather worried as I have not very much experience of social work. Lots of other people seem to know more than me and have worked in social care for years. But I do have two teenage children, a boy and a girl, and their friends often come and tell me their problems. Often my house is like a youth club. Sometimes I try to help my daughter's friends get on better with their parents by helping them to see each other's point of view. I suppose these might be like social work skills. I did the access course at the FE college and spent two weeks on placement in a day centre for older people and I got on with them really well – they were really sweet. The access course helped me get back to reading and now I'm really in to it. Also I learnt how to organise an essay.*

- *I think I will do the reading OK and maybe the writing. But I am not that confident – I'm sure other people will be more clever than me.*

- *I am very anxious about the placements, and real-life clients. I'm a bit worried I may not be able to give them what they need and they might get angry.*

Dan Mitchell (29 years) wrote as follows.

- *I've got bags of social work knowledge and experience – so that is no problem. Been working in family support for years and really just need the academic bit to get the piece of paper that means I can get paid more. I suppose there are parts of social work I don't know so much about – older people and so on. But I know I want to be a children and families social worker.*

- *I feel alright about most of the course – I'm up for it, I think. I like a challenge and usually take things in my stride.*

- *It might be strange having to sit in a classroom all day. I'm used to being out and about in my car – seeing families, supervising contact, and picking up kids, taking young people to McDonald's. I might get restless. I might get impatient if there are people who don't know much and need long explanations. I could get bored. I am a 'doing' kind of person.*

CASE STUDY *continued*

Saranita Khan (19 years) wrote as follows.

- *I bring lots of knowledge from my good A-level results in psychology and sociology. I know these subjects are really important in social work. I also have knowledge of my culture which might be useful to other people on the course. And I know what it's like to be a teenager with problems – I have been a carer for my mother, who has a disability, for six years. So I think I could really help other people in the same position.*

- *The academic study should be Ok for me. I am used to it – I did my A-levels very recently. I have my computer set up at home and love to research and find out more about things.*

- *I am more worried about the other students – most of them will be older than me. The placements might be a problem for me too – I look young for my age and people might think I am still a child. I wonder if I will experience racism ... I did at school. When I was praised by teachers some students made comments about me behind my back – but I knew what they were saying.*

We will return to Nicola, Dan and Saranita, following their learning journeys, throughout the book.

During the course you should, with the help of your tutors, be keeping a personal development plan (PDP). This is a record, unique to you, of your progress as a learner throughout your course. Your answers to the questions in Activity 1.1 could be a helpful way of identifying the areas in which you felt strong and the areas you felt you needed to develop at the beginning of your course. The activity might also assist you in setting some goals or targets for your learning. Revisiting these during the course and reviewing how much progress you have made will help you to become a self-managing and reflective learner. You should find that your college has its own particular format for your PDP.

Using your experience

From the answers given by the students above it is clear that that groups can be very diverse. You will be studying with people from a range of backgrounds, cultures and with a variety of experiences and have the opportunity to learn a lot from them. But the diversity within a group may also be a challenge as you come across people with different perspectives and views on life from yours. Moreover, what you learn on the course may also unsettle you in various ways. While, during the teaching and learning on the course, your life and work experience will be valued in group discussions and tutorials, you will also find that your ideas and assumptions concerning such experiences will be challenged by tutors and other students. You will be introduced to new ideas and different ways of thinking that might undermine what you have taken for granted and unsettle you both personally and professionally.

RESEARCH SUMMARY

Pam Green Lister (2000) and Edwards (1993) draw on research which clearly highlights the huge impact of challenges such as these. The experiences described by   students included:

- *feeling deskilled when they looked back at their previous practice in the light of new knowledge;*
- *experiencing self doubt about their ability;*
- *needing to 'unlearn' some dearly held ideas and ways of doing things;*
- *some tension with family and friends when the students' ideas and understanding changed and developed.*

CASE STUDY

Dan's learning challenge

Dan has been working with children and families for many years. In the college module on social policy, research into the difficulties of bringing up children in poverty (Ghate and Hazel, 2003: Statham, 2007) is discussed. Dan begins to think about some judgemental assumptions he has made about the families he has visited. This makes him feel uncomfortable about himself as he had always thought he tried to be respectful to the parents with whom he worked. Now he sees that he hadn't really considered what the day-to-day lives of the families were like.

Staff teaching on social courses understand that students are likely to be challenged during the course and will provide safe ways for students to examine their thoughts and feelings, together with tutorial support. It is important that students recognise that openness to looking at issues in different ways and having their ideas questioned will assist them in effective learning.

ACTIVITY 1.2

Responding to being challenged

Think about how you respond when your ideas are challenged. Try to answer honestly. Do you:

- *Become defensive about your ideas?*
- *Feel hurt and angry that you haven't been listened to?*
- *Interrupt and argue back before the challenger has had a chance to explain their position?*
- *Agree with the challenge to avoid conflict?*
- *Find it very easy to look at an issue from a different viewpoint?*
- *Find it difficult to put the arguments to defend your position?*

ACTIVITY 1.2 *continued*

- *Take some time to think about the other person's point?*

- *Weigh up the arguments for and against the other person's ideas?*

- *Try to identify the reasons for holding your viewpoint?*

- *Explore why the reasons for holding the viewpoint are important to you.*

Comment

You will see that the answers at the top of the list indicate reluctance to have ideas questioned and tested, while those at the bottom suggest a more open-minded and thoughtful approach. When you consider your answers you might think about whether they indicate that you will find being challenged difficult and if this could be an obstacle to your learning. Some of the activities later in the book will provide you with more opportunities to constructively and reflectively think about your life and employment experiences, especially in Chapter 7.

It can be helpful to have a 'critical friend' to support you with having your ideas and experiences questioned. A critical friend is someone who likes and respects you; who is happy to be a sounding board for your thoughts and ideas; who helps you to be self-questioning; who will be comfortable and confident to challenge you – and with whom you feel safe to explore ideas (Redmond, 2006).

CASE STUDY

Nicola and Mandy

Nicola had already discovered on her access course that some ideas from sociology had challenged her thinking about gender roles – and this had caused some ripples in her generally calm relationship with her partner Kieran. She began to question why, for example, she was always expected to deal with the school, the GP and her daughter's hospital appointments. During her access course she talked a lot with another student, Mandy, who was also accepted on the social work course. They developed their 'critical friendship' and through this explored new ideas identifying how these impacted on them, as well as supporting each other in finding ways to manage this in their everyday lives. They learnt how to challenge each other sensitively and with care – and both Nicola and Mandy knew that they had become more thoughtful through their regular discussions.

Sometimes students find support groups very helpful to their development through the course. This can especially be the case when students have something particular in common, such as discrimination because of sexuality or race either in college or on placement. Sharing experiences and talking them through in a safe setting outside the classroom can provide support, encouragement and ways to take issues forward.

The Black and Minority Ethnic Social Work Student Support Group

At Saranita's college a Black and Minority Ethnic (BME) Social Work Student Support Group was already in existence when she enrolled on the programme. A BME social worker from the local authority facilitated the group and students from all years of the course met regularly, discussed any concerns and successes and learnt from each other. Feedback on general themes was given to the course leader so anything that needed to be taken further could be raised through the course committee. Saranita was really pleased to be able to share some of her anxieties about how she would be able to manage any racism on placement. More experienced students told her what strategies they had used to raise concerns in the placement in a constructive way.

How we learn: surface and deep approaches

Biggs (2003) and Entwistle et al. (2001) draw a distinction between surface and deep approaches to learning. In a surface approach to learning the student wants to get the task over and done, with as little effort as possible, to meet the requirements of the course. Students taking this approach tend to:

- focus on selected facts rather than developing a full understanding;

- list points rather then developing arguments;

- avoid reading beyond the classroom notes and handouts to enhance their appreciation;

- pad out assignments;

- focus on the signs of learning – words used and isolated facts rather than thinking about meanings and relationships.

In contrast, a deep approach to learning involves:

- becoming actively interested in the content of the course;

- becoming aware of your understanding developing while learning;

- focusing on the underlying meaning of ideas, themes and principles;

- trying to appreciate the relationship between ideas and previous knowledge;

- checking evidence and relating it to conclusions;

- thinking abstractly;

- aiming to think deeply.

Entwistle et al. (2001) add a third approach, which they call strategic. Learners with this approach:

- aim to achieve the highest goals;

- manage their time and effort effectively;

- find the right conditions and materials for studying;

- monitor the effectiveness of their ways of studying;

- are alert to the assessment requirements of the course;

- gear their work to the perceived preferences of tutors.

Biggs (2003) and Moon (2005) argue that a deep approach to learning is essential for students to make progress on degree courses. Entwistle et al. (2001) add that the focus on organising study and self-monitoring in the strategic approach are also fundamental to successful study.

ACTIVITY **1.3**

Your learning approach

Consider whether you tend to take a surface or a deep approach to learning and which aspects of the strategic approach could be applied to you.

Comment

Your answer might give you a sense of how you could develop in how you learn. As you progress through the course you will have difficulty with the academic thinking requirements if you have relied on a surface approach to your studies. It is important to note that these approaches are not set in stone or essential parts of your make-up and you have the potential to change and develop – the teaching, assignments and learning experiences on your degree programme will assist you with this. The examples and activities in this book are designed to help you to develop a deep approach to learning.

CASE STUDY

Dan's learning approach

Dan is at risk of taking a surface approach to his learning. He starts the course by seeing it as a means to an end rather than an opportunity to understand more about social work. He does not really expect to enjoy the experience of learning – and only wants to 'get through'. His tutors will be challenging him to move beyond those areas and approaches with which he is familiar – out of his 'comfort zone'.

Biggs (2003) points out that students learn best when they:

- know where they should be going, what they are aiming for;

- are motivated to get there;

- feel free to focus deeply on the task;

- can work in partnership with tutors and other students.

Your studying will proceed more smoothly if you can try to ensure these factors are in place for you. Understanding how you go about studying, being aware of yourself as a learner and monitoring your own development are important as you move through the course. This will be covered more in Chapter 10.

Getting down to studying

In the last part of the chapter we will explore some hints and tips for effective study.

Organising yourself

To study successfully, good organisation is essential and should avoid wasting time. It can ensure that you use your time effectively and are able to keep to the course deadlines.

RESEARCH SUMMARY

This is what some social work students said about studying (SWAP, 2007).

- *Keep on top of deadlines (a diary is a must) and do not let work pile up.*

- *Be meticulous with your recording of notes – date each piece and mark the name of the lecturer/tutor involved.*

- *Just look at what you have to do this week. Break everything down into small tasks. If you look at the enormity of what you have to do it will blow your mind and you'll be discouraged before you start.*

- *Effective time management will mean you can retain a life and not be a victim of your work.*

Here are some tips social work students I have taught found helpful.

Where, when and how to study
- Different people study in different ways. Some people need absolute quiet and some people like to listen to music. Some like to study late in the evening, some prefer to study early in the morning. Some adults like to study while their children are doing their homework – others don't. You need to find out what is best for you.

- Find a space where you can study with reasonable peace and quiet – think about lighting, heating, comfort and potential distractions. Negotiate with other people in your home so that the space you choose is respected.

- Studying effectively for a few hours and taking regular breaks is generally more productive than slogging away unproductively for hours and hours. Some people find it best to study for 30 minutes and take a five- or ten-minute break before returning to the task.

- It will reinforce your learning if you read your notes after a teaching session before filing them away.

- Make sure you find time to relax.

- Reward yourself for keeping to your schedule.

Keep papers and books tidily

- You will be surprised by the amount of books and papers you accumulate over three or four years of study. It is really important to be organised from the start. This will save you time later.

- Find a space for your books and papers. This needs to be a place where they will be safe, organised and where you will easily be able to find what you need. Later in the course you will need to go back to notes and handouts from your first year. You will get very annoyed with yourself if you can't find them.

- Equip yourself with folders, files, sticky notes and paper. File dividers can be helpful.

- Always keep a note of the source of your notes and file your notes away.

- As you go along, try out different systems of organising your growing amount of material.

Time management and making the best use of the time you have for study

It will be difficult to find as much time as you would like to spend on your studies. So making the best use of your time will be very important.

- Each term be aware of the deadlines you have to meet, and work towards them. Note the deadlines in your diary and on your computer.

- Draw up a weekly schedule of goals you need to achieve in the light of the deadlines you have to meet.

- Try to plan to finalise your work a few days before the hand-in date so you are prepared for last-minute crises (such as computer crashes, illness and family crises).

- Prioritise your work carefully – always start with the most important work. If you are unsure about which work is top priority, discuss with your tutor.

- Avoid interruptions if you possibly can.

- Negotiate your study time with your family.

- If you have some small chunks of time, use them productively for tasks you can achieve within that space.

- If you are very tired, but need to use the time you have set aside, carry out tasks that are not too demanding, and save the more difficult tasks for when you are fresh and alert.

- Keep a list of tasks and when one is complete tick it off. This will give you a great sense of achievement.

Looking after yourself

Because the course will be demanding in lots of ways, it is really important to get into good habits of taking care of yourself both physically and emotionally.

ACTIVITY **1.4**

Looking after yourself

Make a list of the steps you can take to look after yourself so you can get the most out of the course.

Comment

In your answers you might have identified the following.

- Eat healthily: your brain will work better if you are eating a balanced diet including fresh fruit and vegetables and food containing omega 3 and 6 fatty acids.

- Eat breakfast: eating breakfast is said to improve alertness and motivation in the morning.

- Drink plenty of water: drinking water can help neural activity in the brain and give you energy.

- Aim to get sufficient sleep.

- Deal with stress constructively: if you are in a state of anxious stress and physically tense, resources are taken away from the brain. Short, brisk exercise can help you move on from this. If you exercise outside, you can benefit from the daylight.

- Take time for yourself and aim to get the study/life balance right.

- Learn some relaxation techniques.

- Use tutorial support to explore issues that are troubling you.

- Have confidence in your ability to learn even if you get stuck and encounter obstacles.

Develop the habit of reading

In order to manage the course successfully you will need to read widely and effectively. One way to build the habit is to read novels or less academic books which deal with issues of relevance to social work. To read effectively, select your reading material with care and learn to skim-read and focus your best energy and attention on the chapters or passages that are relevant to you. Using highlighter pens and sticky notes will ensure you can easily find the passages to which you will need to return.

Use the internet with care

One of the exciting things about the internet is the freedom it gives to people to communicate with others via their web pages. However, this also means that extreme and minority views can be widely circulated. Unlike books and journals which have been subjected to review and assessment by editors, material on a website may not have been through any external scrutiny. So, when you are using website material you need to have an idea of the validity of the material you are using. You need to think carefully about who has produced the ideas and why. For example, there are websites produced by groups of men who have experienced domestic violence. However, statistics tell us that it is mostly women who experience serious domestic violence. So, while the websites express a valid minority viewpoint, any information used from them needs to be put into context within your essay or assignment. There are also many official websites which can helpfully be used to access government reports, policy documents, research and statistics.

C H A P T E R   S U M M A R Y

This chapter has introduced the degree in social work and highlighted some important issues that students need to take into account during their studies. It has given particular attention to the value of the experiences students bring to the course but also how students need to be open to challenge. Some ways of being supported have been identified. Finally, some helpful ideas for studying have been suggested.

By exploring some of the challenges of the degree in social work, this chapter risks alarming and daunting some students. I hope that is not the case and that instead it has captured your interest and excited you about the journey to becoming a qualified social worker. At times you will feel tired and frustrated but, hopefully, more often you will enjoy learning, developing your understanding, becoming more able to explore ideas, concepts and theories and really come to appreciate the joy of studying for your degree in social work.

FURTHER READING

Study skills textbooks
Cottrell, S (2003) *The study skills handbook*. Basingstoke: Palgrave.
Northedge, A (2005) *The good study guide*. Buckingham: Open University Press.
Both these books provide detailed and very helpful advice for studying.

Reading to help you find out more about social work
Reading the journal *Community Care* on a regular basis either in hard copy or via the web page www.community.care.co.uk will give you a sound grasp of current policy and practice issues in social work. It includes reviews of relevant research and often articles present the perspectives of service users.
Horner, N (2006) *What is social work?* Exeter: Learning Matters.
A good readable introduction to social work.
Cree, V and Davis, A (2007) *Social work: Voices from the inside*. Abingdon: Routledge.
This book includes the voices of social workers and of people who use services organised by different settings.

Doel, M and Best, L (2008) *Experiencing social work*. London: Sage.
Includes accounts from people who have used social work services and what practioners can learn from their stories.

Examples of books on social topics.
Hanley, L (2007) *Estates: An intimate history*. London: Granta.
Toynbee, P (2003) *Hard work: Life in low paid Britain*. London: Bloomsbury.

Below are a few examples of novels on topics relevant to social work.
Age
Graham, L (2000) *Dog days, Glenn Miller nights*. London: Black Swan.

Bereavement
Hill, S (1974) *In the springtime of the year*. London: Penguin.
Forster, M (2007) *Over*. London: Vintage Books.

Children

Axline, V (1997) *Dibs in search of self*. London: Penguin.

Doyle, R (1993) *Paddy Clarke ha ha ha*. London: Minerva.

Riley, J (1985) *The unbelonging*. London: The Women's Press.

Disability

Brown, C (1989) *My left foot*. London: Mandarin.

Nolan, C (1987) *Under the eye of the clock*. London: Pan.

Mental health

Frame, J (1980) *Faces in the water*. London: The Women's Press.

Forster, M (1989) *Have the men had enough?* London: Penguin.

O'Farrell, M (2006) *The vanishing act of Esme Lennox*. London: Headline.

Race

Ali, M (2003) *Brick Lane*. London: Transworld Publishers.

Fuller, V (1992) *Going back home*. London: The Women's Press.

Levy, A (2004) *Small island*. London: Headline Book Publishing.

Syal, M (2000) *Life isn't all ha ha hee hee*. London: Anchor.

Chapter 2

Understanding and using concepts and principles: Values and social work

Introduction

The purpose of this chapter is to explore some major concepts and principles which provide the foundation for social work thinking. It aims to provide ways of helping you to grasp what they are and appreciate their relevance.

After reading this chapter you should be able to:

- understand the meaning, in academic terminology, of concepts and principles;

- identify significant concepts used in social work;

- appreciate the main principles of social work;

- recognise how values are integral to social work.

Understanding concepts and principles

Without a good understanding of concepts and principles, and how they are used, it is difficult to take a deep approach to your learning and move on to other stages of the degree. It will be of benefit to you later to invest the time now so as to achieve a sound appreciation of them. In order to support you with this we will explore the meaning of both concepts and principles before considering some examples, using activities to embed your understanding.

First it is worth considering what it means to really understand an issue. Biggs (2003) argues that one level of understanding occurs when people are able to explain something or answer questions on it. This is known as declarative or propositional knowledge. But real understanding changes the way people perceive the world and as a result they do things differently. Over the course of the degree your level of knowledge and appreciation of issues should develop and deepen so that it becomes functioning understanding; you should be able to use your knowledge to decide why, how and in which order to do things and solve problems. In social work this means using your understanding to guide how you go about your practice. In this chapter we are concerned mostly with declarative or propositional knowledge – knowing about things – but because both social work and social work education is about change and transformation, we may also touch upon deeper understandings.

We will first explore the notion of concepts and identify some important social work concepts before exploring some ways of learning to grasp them.

Concepts

A concept has been defined as *a mental representation of a group of items which are similar in some way* (Cottrell, 2003, p163). Alternatively, the *Oxford Dictionary of English Second Edition* (2003) defines a concept as a general notion, an abstract idea. So considering a concept means thinking in an abstract and general way – moving beyond a focus on tangible things. This is a basic and key element of thought in higher education. In order to think in a complex way at the later stages of the degree you will need first to develop your ability to think in a conceptual way.

Cognitive psychologists, whose interest is in how people learn and develop thought, have put forward theories about when and how the ability to think conceptually and abstractly occurs. These tend to focus on the stages of child development: being able to understand concepts is one stage. Piaget called it the stage of formal operations – the last of four.

When this is reached an individual can think abstractly, test problems in the mind and form complex ideas (Ingleby, 2006). Kolb was concerned generally with how people learn – including adults. He argued that learning happens in a cycle and abstract conceptualisation is an important stage in this. Learners move from concrete experiences, to reflective observation, then to abstract conceptualisation before actively experimenting with the new understanding reached (Parker, 2004). We will consider Kolb's ideas in more depth in Chapter 6. For now it is worth noting that moving between concrete and abstract ideas is an important part of the process of conceptual learning. There are a number of important concepts in social work which you will use in your studies and, at later stages of the course, analyse and critically evaluate. In this chapter our focus is on understanding them. First we will name some important concepts in social work, then we will explore two important concepts by moving from the abstract to concrete examples and vice versa.

Concepts in social work

ACTIVITY 2.1

Concepts in social work

Using the definition of a concept (above), list six concepts which you think are important in social work.

Comment

You can find a full list of all the concepts which are relevant to the study of social work in the National Occupational Standards (TOPSS 2002a) and the QAA Benchmark Statement for Social Work (2008). Examples that you might have written down include:

- justice
- care
- need
- poverty
- social exclusion
- prejudice
- institutional discrimination
- accountability
- power
- authority
- emotional well-being.

In the disciplines which inform social work thinking such as sociology, social policy, psychology and law, there are other concepts which you might have mentioned. These are relevant to understanding social work and so you need to be able to discuss them in an abstract and general way, as well as being able to name specific instances.

For example:

- sociology: class, institutionalisation, the state;

- psychology: attachment, resilience, risk;

- law: rights, confidentiality, justice, significant harm;

- social policy: welfare, modernisation, equality.

When reviewing your list, check to see that they all, like those above, are abstract notions or ideas.

In order to better understand concepts we will explore two: social exclusion and power. We will look at each in a different way. When exploring social exclusion we will move from the abstract to the concrete and when considering power we will start with the concrete and work towards the abstract.

ACTIVITY *2.2*

The concept of social exclusion

- *First define social exclusion.*

- *Next list the attributes or characteristics of social exclusion.*

- *Provide some concrete examples.*

Books you could refer to:

Cunningham, J and Cunningham, S (2006) Sociology and social work. *Exeter: Learning Matters (Chapter 3).*

Pierson, J (2002) Tackling social exclusion. *Abingdon: Routledge.*

Gordon, D, Levitas, R and Pantazis, C (2006) Poverty and social exclusion in Britain: The millennium survey. *Bristol: The Policy Press.*

Comment

Compare your answers with the outline below.

Pierson (2002, p7) defines social exclusion as *a process that deprives individuals and families, groups and neighbourhoods of the resources required for participation in the social, economic and political activity of society as a whole.*

Identifying the attributes or characteristics of a concept can help you to develop a better understanding of it. The attributes of social exclusion are:

- it is a process – the way things work in society;

- it occurs because of the impact of structural factors;

- a variety of factors can lead to social exclusion but poverty and low income are significant;

- it happens to a minority of people in society;

- people who experience social exclusion have different life experiences and opportunities from other people.

Finally, we can better appreciate social exclusion by listing some concrete examples of groups who are socially excluded, such as:

- older people feeling isolated in neighbourhoods that are changing rapidly;

- disabled children who cannot access mainstream schools;

- asylum seekers who are unable to access benefits;

- children from families on low wages whose parents can't afford to give them money for the cinema or to go swimming.

In the above example we started from the concept of social exclusion, using abstract thinking, and moved towards concrete examples. Another way of learning to grasp concepts is to begin with concrete examples and work towards a definition.

ACTIVITY **2.3**

The concept of power

- *First think about and write down some* concrete examples *of how social workers exercise power.*

- *Then list the* attributes *of power.*

- *Finally provide a* definition *of power.*

Below are some useful books you could refer to.

Adams, R (2003) Social work and empowerment. *Basingstoke: BASW/Macmillan.*

Beckett, C and Maynard, A (2005) Values and ethics in social work. *London: Sage.*

Cree, V (2000) Sociology for social workers and probation officers. *Abingdon: Routledge.*

Dominelli, L (1997) Sociology for social work. *Basingstoke: Macmillan.*

Payne, M (2006) What is professional social work? *Bristol: BASW/Policy Press (Chapter 6).*

Comment

Now compare your answers to the following.

Some examples of how social workers can exercise power.

- They can be involved in decisions about allocating money, e.g. for children in need (section 17 of the Children Act 1989) and may have budgets to allocate.

- Their assessments of service users can influence decisions about the services they receive.

- They can persuade service users to do things because of their fears that the social worker will use their power under the law.

- Sometimes they have strong personalities and can be very persuasive.

- They are working with people who are vulnerable.

- They know all the social work jargon.

- They are listened to at case conferences or reviews when presenting their assessment of a situation.

- They are well educated.

- They are usually middle class and white.

- They know other professionals and are respected by them.

- They know lots of useful information about how to access services.

The main attributes of power are that it can:

- make things happen;

- be used for good but this is not necessarily the case – it can be used against people;

- be linked to status;

- be about individual personality.

This helps us to define the concept of power as the ability to do or to act: the exercise of authority, influence or control.

The principles and values of social work

Having explored concepts and some ways of grasping them, we will consider the principles of social work. The *Oxford Dictionary of English* Second Edition (2003) defines a principle as *a fundamental truth or proposition that serves as the foundation for a system of belief or behaviour or for a chain of reasoning*. So we can see that principles, like concepts, will require abstract thinking. A consideration of principles also requires us to think about the nature of the profession of social work as distinct from others. The definition of social work used in the National Occupational Standards for Social Work (TOPSS, 2002a) taken from the International Association of Schools of Social Work and the International Federation of Social Workers explains:

> *A profession which promotes social change, problem solving in human relationships and the empowerment and liberation of people to enhance well being. Utilising theories of human behaviour and social systems, social work intervenes at the points where people interact with their environments. Principles of human rights and social justice are fundamental to social work.*

So we can see that the principles of social justice and human rights are basic to social work. The Quality Assurance Agency for Higher Education (2008) *Subject Benchmark Statement for Social Work* requirements state that social work is a moral activity and hence social work education must include a study of ethical principles and values. From its origins social work was based on views of what the profession should be aiming for and how it should be going about it. Some of these have evolved and changed but many remain remarkably similar (Dominelli, 2004).

All social work students are now required to register with the General Social Care Council (GSCC). This means agreeing to uphold the General Social Care Council (2002) *Code of Practice for Social Care Workers*, which sets out the conduct expected of social workers – behaviour which is consistent with a set of values. Hence throughout your course you will be expected to demonstrate these values in both your written work and in your social work practice during your placement.

ACTIVITY **2.4**

The values of social work

Find your copy of the General Social Care Council (2002) Code of Practice for Social Care Workers *(www.gscc.org.uk) . This is set out as behaviour which is expected of social workers. From it put together a list of the values of social work expressed in an abstract way.*

Comment

You might have written the following:

- Respect for people as individuals and promoting
  - self-determination
  - independence
  - dignity and privacy

- Protection from harm

- Rights

- Equal opportunities

- Anti-discrimination

- Respect for
  - diversity
  - age
  - experience
  - different cultures and values

- Responsibility

- Trustworthiness

- Reliability

- Confidentiality

- Empowerment

- Honesty

- Accountability

- Social justice.

You might find slightly different versions of these in social work textbooks but this is a generally agreed list of values.

ACTIVITY 2.5

Service users, carers and values

Find your copy of the Statement of expectations from individuals, families, carers, groups and communities who use services and those who care for them *(TOPSS, 2002)*

Draw out from the whole statement *the values that people who use services consider to be important. Again list them as concepts.*

Compare this list with the one from Activity 2.4.

Comment

In your second list you might have written:

- honesty (this is mentioned several times)

- respect

- inclusion

- reliability

- confidentiality

- accountability

- valuing

- promoting independence

- empowerment

- anti-discrimination.

The two lists you have compared are similar but, as you will have noticed, have different emphases.

Values and your studies

Values will be a consistent theme during your course. They should be integrated into all aspects of your study and thinking. You will need to show that you understand and have incorporated the values of social work into essays, assignments and into your practice when you are on placement. Values will provide you with a way of thinking: criteria for evaluating the theories you are studying, the social work practice you are observing, the social policies you are discussing and the research studies you are exploring. (You will find more on evaluation in Chapter 4).

CASE STUDY

Using values in an essay

Saranita chose to write an essay on the National Service Framework for Older People (NSFOP) (Department of Health, 2001a). She chose this because she had spent three days shadowing a hospital social worker on a ward for older people. She noted that that the NSFOP promotes the values of empowerment and participation which correspond to social work values. But she had noticed that the way older people were treated on the ward did not seem to match up to these ideals. For example, Mrs Christodoulou was presented with information about her discharge from hospital in a rushed and confusing way. Funding constraints meant that another patient, Mr Billson, was not able to go to the residential home of his choice. Saranita thought about what she had seen and checked whether these older peoples' experiences were consistent with the values set out in the NSFOP. She was able to use this thinking in her essay.

The values of social work should guide the language you use in your written work – both at college and on your placement – and of course the language you use with people who use services and colleagues. Your choice of words should be consistent with the values of respect, dignity, empowerment, anti-discrimination, inclusion and social justice. Thompson (2006) explains the important role of language in both constructing and maintaining oppression and discrimination. Gregory and Holloway (2005) illustrate this, showing how the use of the term 'offender' in probation work is a persistent reminder of the 'otherness' of the people with whom the service works and can convey disrespect and the futility of change. But language can also be used in other ways – to create relationships of partnership and responsiveness with people who use services.

RESEARCH SUMMARY

Hawkins et al. (2001) studied Australian social workers' language and found that few terms relating to social justice were used. More often social workers used language that suggested they saw the causes of people's problems as related to individuals. The authors conclude that patterns of terminology used seem to indicate a predominance of clinical and traditional professional language which implies an unequal and distanced relationship with service users (p10). *In the language used there was little sense of the social workers seeing themselves as working together with or alongside families.*

The words you choose to express yourself will convey how you understand the circumstances of the people who use social services and the value you place on them, together with how you see the role and purpose of social work.

ACTIVITY **2.6**

Choice of words

Think about some adjectives used to in relation to families who might be referred to the children and families services of a local authority.

Then consider what messages are conveyed by the terms.

Comment

Some negative terms that I have seen used are:

- problem;

- anti-social;

- dysfunctional;

- inadequate;

- overdependent.

All these seem quite judgemental, conveying the sense that any difficulties being experienced lie within the family or family members rather than with the way society and services are organised – or with the approach taken by the social worker.

Some difficulties with values

Students can find it difficult to thoroughly integrate values in their work. This may be because they have not sufficiently developed their own awareness of the reasons why values are important.

CASE STUDY

Institutional racism

Nicola spent five days shadowing a social worker in a community mental health team in a diverse inner-city area. But she was not aware of, and did not follow up suggestions for reading on, the extent of institutional racism in mental health services (Graham, 2007). Hence it was difficult for her to make sense of her observation that there was a high proportion of men of African Caribbean background on the hospital ward but very few in a hostel for support on discharge. Reluctant to ask, she avoided the issues and did not write about them in the related assignment. When providing feedback on the assignment, her tutor noted that she did not seem to have developed her learning about race and mental health.

Sometime students take a surface approach to values rather than the in-depth approach that studying social work requires, as discussed in Chapter 1. Here are some examples from student assignments I have read.

- It is very important that social workers show respect to the people they are working with.

- When on my placement I worked in an anti-discriminatory way.

- I have found values very useful when thinking about practice.

We can see that these statements do not tell us very much about the students' understanding. The writers have fallen into the trap of making points rather than developing arguments; they have superficially used the relevant language rather than delving deeper and thinking about meanings and relationships. In Chapter 1 we noted these were signs of surface learning. Unless these statements are followed by thoughtful exploration, linked to examples, they demonstrate only that the student knows that it is important to mention values.

CHAPTER SUMMARY

This chapter has introduced the notion of concepts and principles in social work and provided some ways of helping you to grasp these. It has emphasised the importance of a sound appreciation of these as a foundation for future study and indicated the importance of a deep approach to learning for this. These themes will be revisited and developed in later chapters when we particularly think further about using values in reflection, to evaluate research and some of the dilemmas of implementing values in practice.

FURTHER READING

Useful textbooks which generally discuss social work and values

Banks, S (2006) *Ethics and values in social work*. Basingstoke: Palgrave Macmillan.

Beckett, C and Maynard, A (2005) *Values and ethics in social work*. London: Sage.

Parrott, L (2006) *Values and ethics in social work practice*. Exeter: Learning Matters.

Thompson, N (2006) *Anti-discriminatory practice*. Basingstoke: Palgrave Macmillan.

This book has a specific focus on anti-discriminatory social work.

Chapter 3

Relating theory to practice

Introduction

During the first level of their undergraduate degree all students are required to know the underlying concepts and principles associated with their area(s) of study and interpret these within the context of that area of study. For social work students this means, firstly, being able to understand relevant and significant theories and, secondly, being able to explain their meaning and connections to social work thinking and practice. The latter is often described as linking or applying theory to practice; that is, showing how a theory helps to explain different aspects of social work. Students do not always find it easy to make these links. The purpose of this chapter is to support you in developing this academic skill. After reading this chapter you should be able to:

- understand what theory is;

- appreciate the important role of theory in social work practice;

- identify some theories that are significant and relevant in social work;

- make connections between some relevant theories and social work thinking and practice.

Theory and social work

What is theory?

It is important first to be clear what the term theory means in an academic sense. Cottrell (2005, p149) provides a useful general definition:

> *A theory is a set of ideas that helps to explain why something happens or happened in a particular way, and to predict likely outcomes in the future. Theories are based on evidence and reasoning, but have not yet been conclusively proved.*

Thompson's (2000, p22) definition includes similar ideas:

> *An attempt to explain…a framework for understanding…a set of ideas linked together to help us make sense of a particular issue.*

Writing about social work theory, Beckett (2006, p33) makes a connection with practice:

> *…a set of ideas or principles used to guide practice which are sufficiently coherent that they could if necessary be made explicit in a form which was open to challenge.*

We can see then that theories are a grouping of interrelated ideas which have been systematically developed to explain not just how things happen and are connected but also why. They are used to illuminate, or throw light on, our understanding of issues and help us to make sense of the world. They must explain the matter logically and clearly enough for the ideas in the theory to be discussed, criticised or challenged. Thompson (2000) explains that there are different levels of theories. These are:

- grand, macro-level or global theories (sometimes known as meta-narratives), such as marxism or psychoanalysis, which claim to be able to explain everything in society, or all human behaviour;

- middle-range theories which focus on a limited range of issues – for instance, labelling theory, which from a social interactionist perspective aims to explain deviance;

- micro theories developed to explain very small-scale situations – for instance, relationships between staff and patients on a hospital ward.

All academic subjects have a body of theory which explains the issues with which the subject is concerned. Within this there will be a range of competing theories which have different explanations for an issue. Theories will also be contested – there is not necessarily agreement about the merit of different theories. Social work has its own body of theory but has always also drawn on other academic subjects, in particular:

- psychology: the study of mind and behaviour;

- sociology: the study of the relationship between the individual and their social world;

- social policy: the study of the development, implementation and impact of government welfare policy;

- law: the study of the relevant legislative framework and its underpinning principles.

Because of the significance of these subjects, you will find that some social work courses include modules such as applied psychology and sociology for social workers. To a lesser extent social work also draws on medical, political, economic, philosophical and organisational theory (Trevithick, 2005a).

What aspects of social work might theory be used to explain?

Social workers might use theory to understand and explain three main aspects of social work (Sibeon, 1990; Trevithick, 2005a):

- the task and purpose of social work – the role of social work in society;

- practice theories: sometimes called social work approaches or methods – how to go about doing social work;

- the world of service users, including the internal (psychological) world and the external (social) world.

ACTIVITY **3.1**

Issues that theory might explain

Bearing in mind the three points above, make a list of six specific issues in social work that theories might help to explain.

Comment

Below, taken from *The National Occupational Standards for Social Work* (TOPSS, 2002a), you will find some examples of issues which social work students might draw on theories to explain. Check your list against them.

- Policy on social care, criminal justice, education, health, housing, income support.

- Demographic and social trends.

- Poverty, unemployment, health, impairment and other sources of discrimination and disadvantage and their impact on social exclusion.

- Human growth and development and the factors that impact on it.

- Social interactions and relationships.

- Human behaviour.

- How systems work.

- Social work practice.

- The impact of authority and power in the social work role.

- The impact of discrimination.

- Social work with the main groups of people using services.

- Organisations, group behaviour and organisational change.

- Ways of promoting personal, social and emotional well-being.

How might theory be of use?

Social work, like all professions, uses theory to guide practice. Howe (2002) identifies five ways in which this might happen.

- *Observation*: theory provides guidance on what a social worker might need to look out for when meeting people who use services or carers and their families.

- *Description*: theory provides a generally understood and shared language in which these observations can be organised and recorded.

- *Explanation*: theory can suggest how different observations might be linked in a framework that explains them.

- *Prediction*: theory can indicate what might happen in the future.

- *Intervention*: theory can provide ideas about what might bring about a change in the situation.

ACTIVITY **3.2**

Using theory in social work

When shadowing social worker Vicky, Saranita accompanied her on a visit to a residential home for older people. The purpose of the visit was to review how Mrs Lane, an 85-year-old woman, who had been there for four weeks following discharge from hospital, was progressing. Before they went Vicky asked Saranita to think about what theories she had learnt which might help her focus on what she should be observing. This was a challenge to Saranita and she had to think really hard about what she had been taught in college.

What theories do you think Saranita might have identified?

Comment

You (and Saranita) might have identified Erikson's theory of stages of psychosocial development and the related psychosocial crisis of old age – integrity versus despair (Beckett, 2002). You would then be observing whether Mrs Lane seemed to be contented, without regret about her life and had achieved a sense of fulfilment – integrity. On the other hand, you might be looking for signs of despair – frustration with what her life has been like and a feeling that it is too late to change it. This despair might be expressed through unhappiness, or passive helplessness.

You might also have used your understanding of the theory of ageism to be observant about the view of Mrs Lane held by the staff in the residential home. For example, being aware that ageism involved the stereotyping of older people, you might be alert to assumptions being made about Mrs Lane's interests, her life story, her choices and her capacity to make decisions (Thompson, 2006).

Different people reading this might have chosen other theories. It can be useful to think about and reflect on, our preferences for some theories over others and the reasons for this.

In this chapter we will focus particularly on theories which help to explain the world of service users. These have mostly been drawn from other social sciences as discussed earlier. Each of these major disciplines is made up of different 'schools', or ways of thinking about that subject, which provide contrasting ways of understanding a particular issue. For example, psychology offers possible explanations for human behaviour and development and is made up of different schools of thought – behaviourism, humanism, psychodynamic theory, cognitive theory and neurobiological theory (Ingleby, 2006). Sociology deals with the relationship between an individual and their social context; it includes the functionalist, marxist, interpretive, feminist and postmodernist schools (Cree, 2000).

It will be apparent that social work adopts an eclectic approach to theory; it uses theories from different disciplines and so a social worker might draw on a diverse range of theories to explain a situation. Beckett (2006) argues that this is inevitable because there is no one global theory that can explain the complexity of the situations social workers will come across. Sometimes the term 'eclecticism' is used unhelpfully by students and practitioners as a smokescreen for not being clear about the theoretical basis for their thinking. However, skilled and confident students and practitioners should be able to articulate their thinking and practice drawing on a range of diverse theories in a fluent way.

In addition to the formal or official theories, discussed above, social work practice draws on informal 'practice' theories. Formal theories are those which can be found in academic textbooks and will be taught to you on your social work course. Examples would be Marxist theories of poverty; feminist theories of patriarchy; psychoanalytic theories of behaviour. Because this formal theory is set out in academic books, articles and research studies, it can be argued about, debated, explored, analysed, tested, challenged, built on and extended. In contrast, informal 'practice wisdom' theories are the ideas that social workers have developed through their work. They are passed on from experienced staff to new recruits through day-to-day tasks and the culture of the profession. But because informal theory is often not made explicit, recorded or documented it is difficult to challenge or debate. Nor are the assumptions behind it made clear. However, this practice wisdom and reflection can play an important role in developing theories about social work. Formal theory can and should influence practice but social work thinking can also advance through the development of informal theories and reflection on practice (Thompson, 2000; Beckett, 2006). This, together with Schön's (1983) notion of the reflective practitioner, will be discussed in more depth in Chapter 7.

The importance of theory

Theory is important, in social work and social work education, for a number of reasons because it:

- is the mark of a profession;

- can ensure accountability;

- can help avoid discrimination;

- provides a way of making sense of complexity and uncertainty.

The practice of all professions is based on theoretical knowledge which those working in that occupation understand, can relate to the concerns of their area of work and are able to use to explain why they take a particular approach. The important definition of social work adopted by the International Federation of Social Workers in 2000 and used in *The National Occupational Standards for Social Work* (TOPSS, 2002a) states that social work uses *theories of behaviour and social systems and social work is an interrelated system of values, theory and practice* (cited in Beckett, 2006, p5).

Professionals need to have a shared framework for making sense of what they are observing and experiencing and for articulating their practice. In social work this is essential so that practice is not based on individuals' thoughts and views but relies on a common understanding which can be discussed and debated with colleagues. Without theory, *practice will be too limited by personal experience and too dependent on individual assumptions that have not been subjected to a wider professional scrutiny* (Rowlings, 2000, p57).

Theory, then, provides social workers with a means of organising our observations and thinking and a shared basis on which to decide what we should be doing, what is the best way forward and why we have decided this. This means that social workers can articulate and explore with others the principles and thinking on which their practice is based and the reasons for choosing a particular approach. Explaining the theory which has guided practice in a particular direction ensures that underlying and possibly hidden assumptions can be uncovered and made clear. As a consequence the reasons (the 'why') for a particular course of action can be justified. This, in turn, provides a level of accountability to colleagues, other agencies, employers, courts, tribunals, child protection conferences. As Fook (2007, p93) argues, *there is an onus on practitioners to theorise their practice in ways that are accessible to themselves and to the broader profession*. Further, being explicit and clear about the theoretical basis of your thinking and decision-making also provides accountability to the people who use social services and carers. It is an important element of learning to work in partnership with them.

Thompson (2000) further argues that looking beneath the surface, or unmasking, to identify theories needs to happen because it enables hidden assumptions, such as sexism and
ageism, which might justify the continued oppression of groups who have experienced
discrimination, to be highlighted and exposed. Hence appreciating the theories underlying
thinking and practice is essential to ensure that social work is anti-discriminatory.

Another argument for the importance of theory is that, as social work practice becomes
increasingly complex and takes place in unpredictable and uncertain circumstances, theory
provides a way of ensuring we have a way of making sense of the multitude of experiences that social workers go through each day. As Howe (2002, p81) argues, *social
workers face a busy and complex world of human behaviour in a social context. If they
…are to think and act clearly, competently and usefully in practical situations they need to
think theoretically*. Social workers can become caught up in the activity of getting on with
the job and forget the importance of thinking about the theoretical basis of their actions.
However, during your social work training, both in college and when on placement, it is
really important to take the opportunity to take a step back from the hectic world of
everyday practice, to learn and understand the theories of social work and develop your
ability to think theoretically about social work practice.

Theory or procedures?

Some argue that social work practice is becoming dominated by procedures and frameworks rather than being informed by theory (Dustin, 2006; Cree and Davis, 2007). While it
may be true that there has been an increase in policies and procedures, for a number of
reasons this does not mean that theory is irrelevant (Taylor and White, 2000). Firstly, policies and procedures are based on particular theoretical understandings. For example, the
format of the *Framework for Assessment for Children in Need and their Families*
(Department of Health, 2000), widely used in children and families social work, was based
on particular theoretical understanding about what children need to thrive and develop.
The research on which this was based was set out in a related publication (Department of
Health, 2001b), and made available in *The child's world* (Horwath, 2002). Similarly, the
headings used in the Asset assessment tool, used in Youth Offending Teams, were based
on theories, derived from research, about what factors in the lives of young people might
mean they are more or less likely to be at risk of offending (Dugmore and Pickford, 2006).
Other procedures may not have their theoretical underpinning so transparently explained.
Yet, as Thompson (2000) has argued, it can be important to uncover them.

Secondly, theory can help us to understand why there has been a growth in bureaucratic
procedures in social work (and other public services). For example, Parton (1985) used
moral panic theory, developed in the 1960s to understand society's response to 'mods and
rockers' (Cohen, 1973), to explain increased concern about child abuse in the 1970s. He
notes how this new moral panic led to the introduction and growth of bureaucratic procedures concerning child protection, including conferences and registers. More recently,
others have developed a theory of organisations called 'managerialism' to understand the
way in which the organisation of public services including social work changed in the late
1980s and 1990s (Clarke and Newman, 1997). This includes performance management
and the importance of outcomes together with target-setting – known as the 'star rating'

system. Being able to theorise organisational change can help to unearth the reasons for the changes and through this indicate positive ways of working within organisations (White and Harris, 2007).

Can practice be theory-free?

In my experience social work students who have been on practice placements, often return to college and complain that the social workers in their team were not able to identify the theories they were using. This anecdotal evidence is supported by studies of social workers which suggest that they do not always use theory at a conscious level (Secker, 1993; Dustin, 2006). Others have noted that there is a strand of anti-intellectualism in social work that rejects the importance of theory, seeing it as of little relevance to practice (Thompson, 2000). However, as discussed above, behind all thoughts and behaviour are theoretical assumptions which may be hidden but are nevertheless present. As Doel (2000, p162) argues, *theory free professional practice is no more possible than value free professional practice*. This is why you will find on your course that you are asked to be clear about the theories on which you are basing your thinking and practice.

Relating theory to practice

Earlier in the chapter we noted the requirement, at the first level of undergraduate studies, to relate theory to the practice of social work. Each social work programme will have different forms of assessment. However, whatever form they take, you will be tested on your ability to understand principles and concepts (the theories) and interpret these within the context of social work. This might be through an essay, a case study, an assignment or a portfolio of practice learning. You will be expected to show that you understand the links between theory and practice by either:

* explaining a theory and then showing how it might relate to an issue in social work practice;

or

* considering a case study or situation you have come across in social work and showing how theories might help to understand it.

In the next part of the chapter relating theory to practice in both these ways will be explored and examples provided.

Theory and its relevance to social work practice

Before you can make that connection between a theory and practice it is important to first have a clear grasp of the theory. Without this basic understanding it will be difficult to develop your learning. It is like finding a route on a journey – if you don't understand the map, you will not be able to use to it to help you find your way. You can make guesses about the direction you are going in and sometimes you will be right. However, this will be accidental and you will probably find yourself lost again. When you need to use this route another time you will almost certainly find it difficult. In the same way, if you don't have a clear grasp of a theory you will not be able to helpfully use it to make sense of what you come across in social work and, at later stages of the degree, you will find it difficult to be critically analytic of the theory. It is worth investing the time and effort to really grasp new ideas and theories.

When applying theory to practice it may be helpful to go about it in a step-by-step way. The stages set out below may assist you with this.

Stage one: Ensure you have understood the theory

To help you understand and consider a new theory it can be helpful to answer the following questions.

- What is this theory trying to explain?

- What social science and school of thinking does it come from? How has this theory developed?

- What are the basic arguments or main points of the theory?

- Put very simply, how does the theory explain the issue?

If you don't understand the textbook you are using, it can be helpful to go back to a more basic explanation in a different book. However, you should not rely on simpler textbooks but, rather, use them as steps towards understanding books or articles written at the appropriate level for your qualification. Always return to an academic source written at a level appropriate to your stage of study.

Stage two: Outline the theory in your own words

Next, try to explain the theory in your own words. Aim not to use the phrases and words in the books from which you have drawn. It will be a good test of your understanding if you can write it in an original way. If you are stuck, it can be helpful to speak it out loud and write down what you have said. It also can be helpful to try to explain it to another student or even a friend – maybe someone who has little experience of social work ideas. Often teaching something to someone else is a test of whether you have grasped it.

CASE STUDY

Nicola learning to understand theory

Nicola found that though Mandy, her fellow student and 'critical friend,' was really helpful for checking out some issues, when trying to understand theories they just got each other in a muddle. So she asked her partner, Kieran, if it would be alright to get her thoughts together by explaining a theory, in her own words, to him. He was fine with this and it gave Nicola a great opportunity to get feedback on whether she had understood clearly. An unintended, but helpful, consequence was that Kieran felt more involved in Nicola's studies when he had been feeling a bit pushed out by her intense focus on the course.

Stage three: make a connection between theory and practice
Once you have grasped the theory try to think about situations from your own life or from your social care/social work experience that this theory might help to explain.

ACTIVITY 3.3

Attachment theory

Attachment theory, which belongs in the psychoanalytic school of psychology, is used extensively in social work to understand children's emotional development and behaviour. Use the questions and stages above to ensure that you have grasped the theory and can apply it before drawing on the answers below.

You might find the following relatively short chapters a helpful introduction.

Aldgate, J and Jones, D (2006) The place of attachment in children's development. In Aldgate, J et al. (eds) The developing world of the child. London: Jessica Kingsley, pp67–96.

Howe, D (2001) Attachment. In Horwath, J (ed.) (2001) The child's world: Assessing children in need. London: Jessica Kingsley, pp194–206.

For more extended accounts, the following are good sources.

Howe, D (1995) Attachment theory for social work practice. Basingstoke: Palgrave .

Howe, D (2005) Child abuse and neglect. Basingstoke: Palgrave Macmillan.

Comment
Q. What does this theory try to explain?
A. Attachment theory aims to explain how and why children develop relationships with their caregivers and the impact on children's psychological and emotional development if they do not experience satisfactory relationships.

Q. What social science and school of thinking does it come from? How has this theory developed?
A. Attachment theory is a theory from the psychoanalytic school of psychology. It assumes that people's behaviour is the result of interaction between motivation and drives and their environment. Current theory on attachment has evolved from John Bowlby's theories on how children respond when they are separated from their mother. These were developed by Mary Ainsworth, who observed young children with their attachment figures to see how they behaved during separation from the caregiver and when the caregiver returned. From this she devised a classification of types of attachment. David Howe and others have applied the theory to aspects of social work practice.

Q. What are the basic arguments or main points of the theory?
A. The theory argues that the attachment of young children to responsive adults is an important foundation for social competence in teenage and adult life. So, relationships in early childhood are significant for later life. Children need consistent warmth, security, responsiveness and positive, trusted attachment figures in order to develop feelings of

confidence, self-worth, emotional stability and security. Children with a negative experience of attachment figures who are inaccessible, inconsistent, unhelpful or hostile can lack self-confidence and trust, and feel insecure and anxious.

Q. Put very simply, how does the theory explain the issue?
A. People are born with a basic drive towards seeking security and protection from harm through closeness to someone who is seen as stronger and wiser – an attachment figure. While this is true for people of all ages, in later life attachments are usually more reciprocal or mutual. For young children the way caregivers respond to them comes to be their internal working model and from this they develop a sense of how they generally expect people to respond to them.

These are the types of attachment patterns identified.

- Secure attachment: children use their carer as a secure base for exploration. When they are separated they miss them but when they are reunited they are easily comforted and greet the carer with smiles, gestures or words. The carer is alert and responsive to the child.

- Ambivalent or resistant attachment: children are either passive, not exploring what is around them, or they are fretful. They become upset at separation from their carer and will not be comforted when the carer returns. They might then be passive or rejecting of the carer.

- Avoidant attachment: children explore their surroundings, do not respond much when separated from their caregiver and will not be comforted when the carer returns.

- Disorganised attachment: children do not show a consistent response to separation or the carer returning. Their behaviour might be contradictory and include fear, depression and confusion.

Connecting theory and practice

CASE STUDY

Dan connecting theory to practice

When he first started the course Dan was a little sceptical about the value of the theories taught in college. He pointed out that the social workers in the children and families team he had worked in just got on with it, followed procedures and used their common sense. After some teaching on attachment theory his tutor group was given the following question:

What situations from social care/social work might this help me to understand?

He came up with the following answers and began to see how theories might be of use.

- *The different attachment patterns might provide guidance when observing the different behaviours of young children if they are separated from their parents.*

> ### CASE STUDY *continued*
>
> - *The qualities which promote secure attachment could be an important issue to explore when assessing foster parents and people applying to adopt children.*
>
> - *It may provide an explanation for why a young person who has had rejecting, critical parents lacks self-confidence and finds it difficult to trust you.*
>
> *In particular Dan found attachment theory helpful when thinking about his work with 12-year-old Liam who was looked after by the local authority and living with foster carers. Dan knew that Liam had been brought up by his father after his mother died. However hard he tried, Liam had never been able to be good enough at anything for his father, who set very high expectations. Liam had really wanted to please his father but had not succeeded and now had been rejected by him. Liam's foster carers had found it particularly disheartening because when they seemed to be getting closer to Liam, he would do something challenging or difficult which made them feel distant from him.*

Obviously this is a very 'bare bones' outline of attachment theory and on your course you would be expected to use a number of sources and explore the arguments of the theory in more depth. The purpose here was not to provide an extensive debate concerning attachment theory but rather to show how you first need to be able to grasp theory before you start to make the connections to social work.

Using theories to help to understand situations in social work

Now we will explore how you can use theories to make sense of a situation in social work. In order to be able to identify theories that might help you to understand a social work situation or case study, you need to have a 'toolkit' of theories on which you can draw. This means, as discussed above, having a good basic grasp of a range of theories.

In order to be able to think theoretically about a situation it will be helpful to develop a disposition as an active, enquiring learner developing a deep approach to their studies. By this, I mean someone who is:

- motivated to explore an issue;
- open to learning;
- prepared to look beneath the surface and ask questions;
- curious about whatever they encounter;
- keen to understand more;
- able to think deeply;
- willing to have their ideas challenged.

Your lecturers and practice assessors will encourage you to develop good habits of active learning; for example, by making suggestions about exploratory questions to ask when you come across new situations. However, this cannot substitute for taking responsibility for your own personal development as a learner.

Here are some examples of questions you can ask when you are presented with a new situation in social work or a case study.

- What is it important to understand here because of how I feel about the situation? (Your feelings can be a helpful guide to what is important and it will be crucial not to discount them, but to give them careful attention.)

- What is it important to understand here in order to improve the situation?

- What theories might help me understand what is going on and from which disciplines?

- Do I need theories from psychology – which could help explain behaviour?

- Do I need theories from sociology – which could help explain the relationship between the individual and their social context?

- Are there aspects of social policy or law which might help to explain aspects of this situation?

- How well do the theories I have identified help to explain what is going on here? How has it helped my understanding to have used theory to explain these issues?

ACTIVITY 3.4

William Daley

Use the questions set out above to try to link theory to practice in this case study before reading the suggested answers below.

William Daley (30 years old) was in a car accident for which someone else was held responsible. His injuries were so serious it was necessary to amputate his right leg and he also lost some use in his right arm. Prior to the accident William worked as a physical education teacher in a primary school and was a keen amateur footballer. He has been in hospital and a rehabilitation centre for six months. You are a student social worker in the hospital social work team and your role is to support him in moving back to live as independently as possible. Whenever you meet with William he seems to become angry very quickly. Despite your best efforts at supportive communication he often shouts at you. This makes working with him, to make plans for his return to the community, very difficult.

The medical staff seem to be concerned only with the healing of the wounds, how well the artificial leg fits and how much mobility he is regaining. You have been keen to work as a multi-disciplinary team with the medical staff but you often end up feeling as if you do not have a shared focus.

Your aim is to support William and to support him in a move from the hospital but you feel as if you are making very slow progress.

Comment

Q. What is it important to understand here because of how I feel about the situation?
A. You are feeling upset and hurt by William's apparent anger with you although you still want to work with him. These strong feelings could be getting in the way of effective

work with William and so it will be important to develop an understanding of them. Further, you are frustrated by the difficulty of working in a multidisciplinary team.

Q. What is it important to understand here in order to improve the situation?
A. It will be important to understand why the medical team has a different focus from you and why it is difficult to work in partnership with them. Otherwise there is a risk that you become critical of them, which will make joint working more difficult.

Q. Do I need theories from psychology – which could help explain behaviour?
Do I need theories from sociology – which could help explain the relationship between the individual and their social context? Are there aspects of social policy or law which might help to explain aspects of this situation?

A. From psychology, the 'stages of loss' theory might help to understand William's anger. Briefly put, this theory argues that people who have experienced any kind of bereavement or loss move through four stages before coming to terms with their loss (Payne, 2005; Nicolson, et al., 2006; Weinstein, 2008). In relation to loss and disability the stages are said to be shock, denial, anger and depression (Oliver and Sapey, 2006). Currently William is experiencing significant losses – of one limb, partial use of another, his role and employment as a teacher and his identity as a physically active man.

From sociology, theory about different models of disability, medical and social, might help you to understand how the medical team have different priorities for William from social work staff. The medical model of disability sees the causes of the difficulties experienced by the individual as to do with the individual and their impairment. This might be the approach that the medical team has taken. Their concern might be a detailed understanding of the nature of the injuries and their impact on William's ability to achieve rehabilitation. In contrast, the social model focuses on the social, economic and political barriers to people with impairment fully participating in society. It does not see disability as an individual limitation but the outcome of constraints imposed by society (Barnes et al., 2002).

Q. How well do the theories I have identified help to explain what is going on here? How has it helped my understanding to have used theory to explain these issues?
A. William's anger might be understood as a normal stage which he will need to go through before he adjusts to his situation rather than his being dissatisfied with you and your work with him. Understanding William's anger as a stage might mean you could appreciate that this anger may not be a permanent feature of William's personality. It might suggest that he will enter a stage of depression before he is able to come to terms with the losses he has experienced. In addition, it might also help you to think about what social work approaches are likely to be most helpful to support him through this.

It is possible that the team working with William are operating from different perspectives on disability; the medical staff from a medical model and the social work staff from a social model. This can often be the case in multi-disciplinary teams and need not prevent the team from working effectively together. A theoretical understanding of this, however, can help you to appreciate the differences and think carefully about how best you can work together in William's interests.

These are clearly not the only theories which could help to understand William's situation. For example, Erikson's theory of stages of psychosocial development could be used to consider the relevant stage for William (young adulthood), the related psychosocial crisis (intimacy versus isolation) and what this might mean in his current circumstances (Trevithick, 2005a). Goffman's (1961) sociological theories about institutions and institutional behaviour might help explain William's anxiety about leaving hospital, expressed in anger, and the possibly narrow perspective of medical staff.

While we can see how theories can provide ways of helping to understand some aspects of William's situation, it is also important to consider their limitations. Just because a theory is set out in a textbook does not mean it has not been or cannot be criticised. There are disagreements about most theories. For instance, the stage theory of loss we have used above to explain William's anger has been contested. The main points of criticism are that:

- the theory assumes everybody must go through all the fixed stages in order to achieve adjustment;

- the theory focuses on the individual disabled person and neglects the impact of wider contextual issues such as family, community and society;

- many people's experiences are not accounted for by the theory;

- loss is more complex than the theory allows for;

- there are competing theories which suggest that after loss, the way people reconstruct meaning depends on contextual factors – not preset stages.

(Oliver and Sapey, 2006)

A major criticism of traditional theories from social science is that they have been developed from a white male, able-bodied, middle-class and eurocentric perspective, and hence may not adequately explain issues in a diverse and stratified society made up of both men and women (Williams, 1989; Robinson, 1995; Abbott et al., 2005). Neither can theories determine or dictate what a social worker's approach to practice might be – each situation is unique and the individuality of the service user should be an essential factor in planning how to proceed. Theory must be coupled with values, reflection, analysis and a critical stance. In your studies at higher levels of the degree you will be required to take a more analytic, critical and reflective approach to theories and this will be explored in later chapters, particularly Chapters 5 and 11.

C H A P T E R   S U M M A R Y

This chapter has highlighted the requirement that social work students during the first level of the social work degree should be able to apply relevant theories to the concerns and practice of social work. To assist you in this it has clarified what theory is, how everything has theoretical foundations and the important role played by theory in social work. Frameworks for applying theory to practice and understanding practice situations theoretically have been suggested and some examples provided.

Despite its importance, you will be aware that using theory is not the only component of effective practice. Other essential ingredients are knowledge of procedures and legislation; the integration of values; learning from the knowledge and experience of people who use services; working in a skilled manner; using research to inform practice: and building practice; wisdom through reflection. However, being able to relate theory to practice as discussed in this chapter will provide you with an important foundation which can enhance your understanding of the other aspects of practice and on which you will need to build at a later stage in your studies. In Parts Two and Three these issues will be developed further.

FURTHER READING

Beckett, C (2006) *Essential theory for social work practice*. London: Sage.
In Part 1 Chapters 2 and 3 Beckett explores the importance of theory in social work.

Trevithick, P (2005) *Social work skills: a practice handbook*. 2nd edition. Maidenhead: Open University Press / McGraw-Hill.
Chapter 1 provides a useful summary of the theories relevant to social work and a helpful discussion about types of knowledge.

Thompson, N (2000) *Theory and practice in human services*. 2nd edition. Maidenhead: Open University Press / McGraw-Hill.
This book is useful for a more in-depth discussion of the relationship between theory and practice although, as the title suggests, it covers the human services generally – not only social work.

Chapter 4

Writing academically: Evaluation, developing arguments, avoiding pitfalls

Introduction

This chapter is about the skills needed in written assignments at level C of the degree in social work. Assignments will be designed in different ways depending on the course. However, in all written forms of assessment you will be required to present ideas clearly using language appropriate to academic study. Assignments will also test your ability to evaluate both quantitative data and qualitative concepts and to explain your thinking in structured arguments. After reading this chapter you should be able to:

- improve your ability to present your thinking clearly;

- appreciate how to evaluate concepts and data;

- understand how to develop structured and coherent arguments;

- know how to avoid some pitfalls in writing academically.

Aspects of writing

Some social work students are familiar with writing reports and case notes in their previous employment, are articulate in classroom discussion and debate but find it difficult to convey their ideas in writing.

CASE STUDIES

Dan

When he started his social work degree Dan found that he really enjoyed discussing ideas and sharing his experiences in teaching sessions. However, when he started to write his first essay he found it much harder than he had imagined. He knew what he wanted to say and could explain this to his tutor – but getting the words on paper was much more difficult. He was really disappointed with the mark and feedback from his first essay and thought about giving up the course. His tutor encouraged him to work systematically on organising and developing his writing and the effort and time Dan put into this really helped him. Later when he was on a placement in a Children Looked-After Team he was expected to write complex reports. He noticed that the skills he had learnt on the course greatly improved his report writing.

Saranita

Saranita, who had been very anxious about placements, had her confidence boosted by her ability to organise her recordings clearly. She had learnt some of these skills during her A-level studies and built on them during her social work course, before she started her placement.

Dan and Saranita learnt a useful lesson, that some skills, which may appear to be purely academic, can be used in other settings. These are known as transferable skills. Many skills you will develop and use in college will be helpful to you on placement.

When thinking about writing it can be helpful to be clear about different kinds of writing and their purposes. At this level of the degree you are expected to be able to use descriptive and evaluative writing and to be able to put forward a developed argument. In the next part of the book (Chapter 5) we will explore how to write in a critical and analytic way.

Descriptive writing

Descriptive writing is needed to give important and relevant background information so the rest of the written piece of work makes sense. It is normally best to keep this to a minimum so that you have plenty of words left for other more complex types of writing. Descriptive writing is used to:

- give information;
- list detail;
- state what something is like;
- give the order of events;
- explain what a theory says;
- set out the approach used;
- say when something occurred;
- list different aspects of a situation;
- state different options;
- explain connections between items.

In essay titles or the instructions for assignments, the words 'outline', 'explain', 'present', 'state' or 'describe' indicate that what is expected is descriptive writing. This is often required so tutors can assess whether you are able to identify and understand the main aspects of an issue. Because, when studying for a degree, you are expected to do more than describe, it is generally followed by an instruction to write in a different way – often to evaluate or criticise.

CASE STUDY

Nicola's assignment

An assignment given to students on Nicola's course had to be completed after the experience of shadowing a social worker for five days. It included the following questions.

1. Briefly describe the agency; its history; its current objectives; relevant legislation; its service users; the role of the social worker.

2. What evidence did you observe of inter-agency working? What were the positives and the problems of inter-agency working in practice?

From this assignment we can see some of the uses of descriptive writing. In question 1 students are asked to provide background information about the agency and explain the main features of the agency, either from books or from talking to social workers. Question 2 first asks the students to outline what they observed. However, in the second part, students are asked to think more deeply, and to evaluate, by considering the strengths and weaknesses of inter-agency practice. We will discus evaluation next in this chapter.

Nicola shadowed a social worker in a Community Mental Health Team. Here are her answers to Question 1 – an example of descriptive writing.

The agency where I shadowed a social worker was the city Community Mental Health Team (CMHT) which is part of an NHS Mental Health Trust. The team is based in a psychiatric hospital but mostly works in the community. Its main objective is to offer support to and improve the well-being of people experiencing mental health problems. The service users are anyone over the age of 18, who has had an assessment of their mental health problems, been diagnosed with a mental illness and admitted to hospital or is being treated as an out-patient at home.

The team is part of the development of community care, a policy introduced with the closure of large long-stay psychiatric hospitals, or asylums, in the late 1980s and 1990s. At this time it was felt that these hospitals were not the best environment for people with mental health difficulties and could lead to their becoming dependent and institutionalised. This policy has been criticised for not providing enough care and not always safeguarding the safety of the community.

The team uses the Care Programme Approach (CPA) which aims to assess the needs of someone with mental health problems, agree a care plan, provide a key worker and review the plan regularly. The team also offers psychological therapies such as counselling and training in skills in coping with depression. It can provide advice on housing, benefits and employment if needed and psychiatrists might prescribe medication.

The legislation which sets out the responsibilities and powers of social workers is the Mental Health Act 1983. It covers the admission of people to psychiatric hospital against their will, their rights while detained, including being discharged from hospital, and the after care they receive.

The role of the social worker in the team is to be part of the multi-disciplinary team, to contribute to the assessment and care planning process; to advocate on behalf of service users; to support them in dealing with social problems such as benefits or housing and to liaise with a wide range of voluntary organisations.

Some social workers are Approved Social Workers (ASWs) which means that they are involved in decisions about whether someone should be detained under the Mental Health Act 1983.

ACTIVITY *4.1*

Recognising descriptive writing

Identify which parts of Nicola's answer correspond to the features of descriptive writing listed above.

Descriptive writing might also be used to outline or summarise the main features of a theory or social work approach. For example, consider the following essay title:

Outline and critically evaluate advocacy and its contribution to empowerment in social work.

If you had chosen this essay title you would begin with descriptive writing to set out the main aspects of advocacy. But you will see that the second part of the question requires you to make an assessment of advocacy and how much it enables people who use services to be empowered. This would require you to use evaluation skills. When planning the structure of this essay it would be important to plan carefully the allocation of words so you ensure a good balance between description and evaluation.

ACTIVITY **4.2**

Descriptive writing

List, using bullet points, the main descriptive points you would include in this essay about advocacy. To be able to identify these points you should draw on several textbooks and articles. For example:

Coulshed, V and Orme, J (2006) Social work practice. *4th edition. Basingstoke: Palgrave (Chapter 3).*

Trevithick, P (2005) Social work skills: A practice handbook. *2nd edition. Maidenhead: Open University Press / McGraw-Hill (Chapter 7).*

Adams, R (2003) Social work and empowerment. *3rd edition. Basingstoke: BASW/ Macmillan.*

Forbat, L and Atkinson, D (2005) Advocacy in practice: the troubled position of advocates in adult services. British Journal of Social Work, *35 (3), 321–335.*

You might also draw on material from an advocacy project, for example VOICE, www.voiceyp.org

---

Comment

Here are some points you might have mentioned.

Advocacy includes the following aspects.

- Representing the views of someone or a group unable to do so themselves.

- It links to the values of rights and participation: the right of all people to participate in definitions of need and decisions about how those needs may be met.

- It connects to the value of empowerment. The client/service user should have a voice; should be part of decisions made about them; should have the means of challenging decisions made about them; should be enabled to develop skills and assertiveness so they can exercise their own voice.

- It acknowledges that, because of structures in society, some people have less power and access to resources and opportunities. They may therefore have difficulty in having their voice heard.

- It can be about speaking, writing, acting or arguing on behalf of others.

- There are five types: case advocacy; cause advocacy; self-advocacy; peer advocacy and citizen advocacy. Social workers are most likely to be involved in case advocacy: advocating on behalf of another person for resources, services or opportunities, but they might refer service users to other advocacy organisations and groups.

When you are using descriptive writing you will find that it is important to:

- aim to write clearly and succinctly so that you don't take up too much of an assignment with description;

- focus on the most relevant aspects of the issue you are describing – this means you will need to appreciate what is important and, from your reading, be able to pull out the main and most essential points;

- keep a clear focus – not drifting off the point;

- think about the most helpful order in which to present the information.

Evaluative writing

To evaluate means to weigh up or assess, to look for the strengths and weaknesses, the positives and the negatives. Other evaluation words you might find in assignment titles are 'appraise', 'compare and contrast'. In your assignments you might be asked to evaluate an experience, an argument, a theory, social work approach, a policy, an issue or a set of statistics. This will involve making a judgement about the worth, usefulness or validity of what it is you are evaluating.

CASE STUDY

Nicola's assignment – (continued)

If we return to Nicola's assignment we can see that in the first part of question 2 she is asked to describe her observations. The second part gives Nicola the opportunity to evaluate her observations by asking her to outline the positives and the problems of inter-agency working. Here are Nicola's answers, which demonstrate descriptive writing followed by evaluative writing.

2. What evidence did you observe of inter-agency working? What were the positives and the problems of inter-agency working in practice?

The Community Mental Health Team (CMHT) is itself a multi-disciplinary team made up of professionals from a number of different backgrounds: occupational therapists, psychiatrists, support workers and community psychiatric nurses. But the CMHT also works with a number of different agencies, with which people with mental health difficulties might come into contact, for example the police, or agencies from whom they need assistance such as the housing department, the benefits agency or voluntary organisations like MIND and the advocacy service. I noticed that there were regular telephone calls between the social workers and workers from other agencies; sometimes the service users did not know about these phone calls. Sometimes there were arguments between the social workers and other workers. For example, I heard a long dispute between a social worker and the housing department about whether a mental health service user was entitled to emergency accommodation. On another occasion I heard a different social worker almost gossiping about a service user, M., with a day centre worker. They were laughing about his efforts to find a woman friend.

The positives of inter-agency working were that, if all agencies communicated well and worked together efficiently, the service user could have all their needs met. This would mean staff from different agencies listening to each other properly, not stereotyping each other, keeping in good communication and ringing back when they say they will and respecting each other's knowledge. I saw this happen once or twice.

But there were also problems. Sometimes, because the system is quite complicated, service users were very confused about who should be doing what – they didn't always appreciate the roles of each worker and got frustrated when they felt they were going round in circles. One service user told me she had been very distressed by this. I also thought that workers from different agencies could 'gang up on' service users like in the joking I mentioned earlier. This would have a negative effect on service users.

Criteria to use when evaluating

When evaluating you need to use criteria or principles to help you weigh the issues. These might be:

- relevant theorie

- research evidence

- statistics

- social work values

- your observations

- the perspectives of service users and carers

- personal experience.

Some of these will carry more weight than others. For example, while the use of personal experience is valued on social work courses, and can convey powerfully aspects of real life, it represents the understanding of one person. In comparison, a piece of research might have carried out a survey of 1,000 people and have breadth – though not depth.

Criteria for evaluation

Identify the criteria Nicola used to evaluate inter-agency working.

Comment

- First, Nicola used her observations, and her feelings of discomfort about some things she observed, as evidence for her evaluation.

- But she also weighed up what she saw of inter-agency working against her understanding of the values of social work. She was concerned that some people who used the services were not being respected. For example, she had thought carefully about confidentiality and whether this was being observed; she wondered if workers from different agencies were sharing information about service users without them knowing. It would have strengthened her assignment if she had specifically referred to the value of confidentiality.

- Nicola also used what the service user said about her experience of inter-agency working. She could have strengthened this by referring to the *Statement of expectations from individuals, families, carers, groups and communities who use services and those who care for them* (TOPSS, 2002b), which says that, when they are working with other professionals, social workers should be honest, clear and make sure that everybody understands what would happen to information that is shared; why it is shared and how it might be used.

Nicola was asked to consider positives and problems to help her to evaluate. Here is a fuller list of questions that you could use.

- What were the strengths?

- Why are these strengths?

- What were the weaknesses?

- Why are these weaknesses?

- What was not covered; what gaps are there?

- Were aspects of social justice considered?

- What aspects of social justice were not taken into account?

- Were the values of social work integrated?

ACTIVITY **4.4**

The essay on advocacy

We noted that the essay about advocacy asked you to Outline and critically evaluate advocacy and its contribution to empowerment in social work.

In order to develop your evaluative thinking, list three strengths and three weaknesses of advocacy as a social work approach which might contribute to empowerment. To do this you should expand your reading and use examples from your own experience, personal or professional. It would also be important to include what people who use services say about advocacy. It might be useful to use the Statement of expectations from those who use services and carers *(TOPSS, 2002b) as a starting point.*

Comment

Below are some points concerning the strengths of advocacy you might have identified.

- Advocacy could bring in to the mainstream the voices of people who are often marginalised or socially excluded and make sure they were heard.

- A skilled social worker who listens and works carefully with a service user can support them in developing skills and confidence to speak for themself. This growth in self-esteem could have a really positive impact on the rest of their life.

- Social workers who really listen to the voices of service users might learn and understand more about what it feels like to be disempowered.

The following are some points concerning the weaknesses of advocacy you might have identified.

- There is a danger that social workers put their own views forward, not those of the service user.

- There is a risk that an advocate takes over and does all the talking so the service user is disempowered rather than empowered.

- Social workers may find that representing the views of service users puts them in conflict with their own organisation and so they have split loyalties. Because they are not truly independent they cannot really speak on behalf of service users, resulting in them not being properly heard. Service users say that at times it is more appropriate for independent advocates to be involved.

We will return to this later in the chapter.

Evaluating data

You will find that you also need to be able to evaluate data presented to you. This will often be presented in the form of a table of statistics.

ACTIVITY 4.5

Evaluating statistics

- *Study the set of figures below relating to children subject to a child protection plan.*
- *Outline the information contained in the figures.*
- *Evaluate the usefulness of the statistics.*

ACTIVITY **4.5** *continued*

Children who became the subject of a Child Protection Plan (CPP)[1] by category of abuse.

Years ending 31 March 2003 to 2007
Coverage: England
Category of abuse   *Numbers and percentages*

	2003	2004	2005	2006	2007	2003	2004	2005	2006	2007
Neglect	11,700	12,600	13,200	13,700	14,800	39	41	43	43	44
Physical abuse	5,700	5,800	5,500	5,100	5,100	19	19	18	16	15
Sexual abuse	3,000	2,800	2,700	2,600	2,500	10	9	9	8	7
Emotional abuse	5,400	5,700	5,700	6,700	7,800	18	18	19	21	23
Mixed/not recommended by 'Working Together'	4,400	4,300	3,700	3,300	3,200	15	14	12	11	10

Source: CPR3

1. Where a child was made the subject of a child protection plan (registered) more than once in the year within the same authority, each registration has been counted. These include unborn children.

Source : www.dcsf.gov.uk

Comment

In your description of the figures you might have made the following points.

- Overall there has been an increase in the numbers of children who became the subject of a Child Protection Plan (CPP) between 2003 and 2007, except in 2005 when there was a slight drop.

- More children are subject to a CPP because of neglect than for the other categories of abuse.

- There has been a steady increase in the proportion of children subject to a CPP under the categories neglect and emotional abuse.

- There is a pattern of a drop in the numbers of children subject to a CPP under the categories physical abuse and sexual abuse.

In your evaluation of the statistics you might have made the following points.

Some strengths of the statistics.

- They are set out clearly.

- Percentages are given as well as numbers – this provides a better indication of overall trends.

- It is possible to see the trends over five years.

Some weaknesses of the statistics.

- Some important contextual information is missing – it is important to know that the definition of emotional abuse changed and expanded in 2006 when the revised *Working together to safeguard children* (DfES, 2006b) was published.

- The combining of the categories *Mixed/Not recommended by 'Working Together'* could leave a lot of unanswered questions.

- Unborn children are not listed separately, so the reader does not know how many of these are included in the figures.

- These figures do not include race, gender, age, socioeconomic status or geographic distribution.

In order to identify the first two weaknesses you would need to build on your prior knowledge of the history of safeguarding children. To have thought of the third and fourth points you would need to have asked the questions: *What is missing? What are the gaps?* To identify the fourth point you would have needed an awareness of aspects of social justice and inequality. This demonstrates that background knowledge, a systematic approach to evaluation and a strong awareness of relevant issues are all needed.

CASE STUDY

Dan using research and his experience to evaluate

When Dan was given this assignment he came up with an additional point based on his own experience of working in a children and families team.

> I have noticed that sometimes, at child protection conferences, social workers find it difficult to define and provide evidence for emotional abuse and so they seem to focus on other categories.

Dan also read a research article which explored the variations in periods of time that children's names were on child protection registers (Pugh, 2007). This provided him with material to strengthen his argument. The article outlined major differences in registration patterns in local authorities in England and Wales, explored some potential reasons and consequences and identified possible improvements in the collection of data. Using research material in evaluation will be discussed in more depth in Chapters 8 and 9.

Developing an argument in a structured and coherent way

For students new to academic writing it will help you to present your evaluative thinking if you develop the skill of putting your arguments in a structured and coherent way. Below are some important aspects of this.

Build your argument in stages

- Start off by indicating what your overall conclusion is.

- Then set out the points which support your conclusion. For each of your points explain the evidence you have drawn on to support it. You will need to indicate where the evidence is drawn from and be confident that it has validity.

- Next, set out some points that provide a different point of view to your conclusion. Again you should explain the evidence you have drawn on, its sources and its validity.

- Now that you have set out both sides of the argument and the supporting evidence, explain clearly why you have chosen one view rather than another.

- Try to ensure that the points you make follow logically from each other so that the reader can follow your argument.

It can be helpful to aim for paragraphs of roughly equal length, each containing a main theme, as this can break up the text of an assignment into manageable ideas. When you become more confident with academic writing you might vary their size but paragraphs rarely contain fewer than two or three sentences. Aim to avoid long, confusing sentences; it can be helpful to divide them up into two shorter ones. Try not to make too many points in one sentence. Another way to avoid lengthy sentences is to think about whether you can make your point equally well using fewer words.

Use signposting and linking words

Signposting means telling the reader where you are going with your argument. Particular words can help you to both link your ideas together and signal to the reader where your argument is going.

Below are some useful examples of words and how they can help you construct your argument.

- *Also; in addition; then; together with; moreover:* indicate you are adding to a point already made.

- *For example; in other words; for instance; namely; particularly; as follows:* can be used to introduce examples.

- *In contrast; on the other hand; in comparison; conversely; alternatively; although:* signpost that you are introducing a different argument.

- *Therefore; hence; it can be seen that; so; consequently; we can see then:* are used to introduce the result of something.

- *In short; overall; to summarise; therefore; in brief:* show that you are summarising.

- *In conclusion; to conclude; thus:* are terms to introduce the conclusion.

Write clearly

It is important to develop the skill of writing using your own words and in formal but straightforward and clear language. Putting ideas in your own words will show the reader that you have understood what you have read. It is important to avoid using colloquial or informal slang which you might use in everyday conversation. You will need to use professional terminology from social work but be cautious about using jargon expressions which you have not explained, and aim to avoid unnecessary shorthand. Always use language that conveys the values of social work and so avoids bias, discrimination and oppression as discussed in Chapter 2. Beckett and Maynard (2005) observe that although social work claims to be anti-oppressive, often language found in social work files can be derogatory. Terms such as 'victim' and 'dysfunctional', which are regularly used, convey negative messages and hence can construct a harmful view of the people described in this way. To check the clarity of your writing it can be helpful to read it out loud to yourself a day or so after you have finished the draft. This can help you to pick up basic errors and ensure it makes clear sense.

Referencing

To enable the reader of your essay or assignment to check out the sources of your argument you need to provide references. This will make it clear that you are not claiming that someone else's ideas are your own. You also need to provide a list of these sources you have used at the end of the essay/assignment. You should follow the referencing system which your course specifies.

It is really helpful, and will save a lot of time, if you are organised and systematic about referencing from the beginning of your studies. Whenever you are working on an assignment it is helpful to open a new document in which you will list the references you have used. When you are working on your assignment and you include a reference, add it to your list straight away. If you are including a quotation from the book or article, note the page number. As you proceed through the course, you might also find it useful to build up an overall list of references of all the sources you have used. This can be helpful when you want to return to a book or article you have read before.

Making sound judgements

After evaluating or weighing up arguments or theories you will then need to come to a conclusion or make a judgement or a conclusion about the issues you have been exploring. This should include your informed opinion which follows logically from the points you made earlier.

ACTIVITY **4.6**

Coming to a judgement

Return to the essay on advocacy. Look at the list of strengths and weaknesses and write a brief summary in which you come to a judgement about the contribution of advocacy to empowerment.

Comment

Below is a possible answer.

The voices of people who need to use services are often not well heard or put to the forefront of discussions about them because they are vulnerable, unwell, young, old or poor or socially excluded in some other way. Ideally advocacy could make a significant contribution to remedying this situation. However, for social workers it can be a difficult approach to take because of split loyalties and then truly empowering advocacy may not occur. To ensure that advocacy works to empower service users it may need to be provided by an independent organisation. Social workers need to be aware of such advocacy projects and refer service users to them.

Some pitfalls in writing academically

Plagiarism

Plagiarism is using the work of other people without acknowledging the source of your information or inspiration. It is treated very seriously as it is regarded as a form of cheating. Plagiarism can include the following.

- Lifting verbatim (word for word) wholesale written material from books and articles without acknowledging the source. If you are going to use the author's exact words, you must indicate that this is a direct quote. It is not acceptable to use the author's words, change a few and include it in your essay or assignment as if you had written it.

- Rewriting or paraphrasing passages from books and articles without acknowledging the source. It is important always to reference the books and articles which you have used to present information or make an argument.

An example of plagiarism would be taking this extract from Beckett (2002) and putting it into your essay as if you had written it yourself.

> *The stereotype of adolescence in this culture is that it is a stormy time characterised by unreasonable behaviour and rebellion. While few who deal with adolescents would dispute that there is some basis in reality for this stereotype, it is interesting that many researchers who have looked into this have come to the view that it tends to be exaggerated.*

To avoid plagiarism you can indicate clearly that this is a direct quotation by using appropriate referencing and inverted commas as follows.

> *'The stereotype of adolescence in this culture is that it is a stormy time characterised by unreasonable behaviour and rebellion. While few who deal with adolescents would dispute that there is some basis in reality for this stereotype, it is interesting that many researchers who have looked into this have come to the view that it tends to be exaggerated' (Beckett, 2002, pp122–3).*

or

Beckett (2002) argues that:

> *'The stereotype of adolescence in this culture is that it is a stormy time characterised by unreasonable behaviour and rebellion. While few who deal with adolescents would dispute that there is some basis in reality for this stereotype, it is interesting that many researchers who have looked into this have come to the view that it tends to be exaggerated' (pp122–3).*

Or you can put the ideas into your own words. This is generally a much better way of writing, as it shows you have read and understood Beckett's argument and can reword it.

> *Chris Beckett (2002) argues that while a generally held view is that adolescence is an unsettled stage of life marked by challenging behaviour, this is not backed up by research.*

Other ways of avoiding plagiarism include:

- developing the habit of making notes in your own words;

- keeping a very careful note of the source of your arguments and ideas so you don't inadvertently use the author's words;

- referencing your written work fully – then you will be sure that you have shown the sources you have used.

Not building on feedback from previous assignments

There is evidence that using feedback from written assignments is very significant in effective learning. However, students tend to focus only on the grade they have received and not read the written comments. If they read them they may not understand them and often do not act on them (Burke, 2007). While you may find your tutor's comments distressing – one student told me she had thrown hers across the room in disappointment – it will be helpful to return to the feedback when you are calm and identify what you can learn from it. Check that you understand what your tutor has written. If you don't, ask to meet with them so you can discuss it. Pick out the major themes in the feedback and think about what steps you need to take to improve in these areas.

Silly mistakes

Always leave yourself enough time to read through and check your work before you hand it in. This space and distance can help you to see errors that you were not able to see earlier because you were too 'close' to the assignment. Some space can help objectivity. Aim to read through in different ways: first ask yourself if it makes sense, then look only for spelling errors; then just check for grammar and punctuation and finally for referencing.

When checking for sense, questions you can ask yourself include the following.

- Do my sentences convey what I want to say?

- Have I 'signposted' the essay, i.e. have I indicated to the reader where I am taking them throughout the essay?

- Are the paragraph breaks in the right place?

- Is the argument put together in a way that makes sense?

It can be useful to find a friend to help with this as, seeing it for the first time, they may be more able to look at the assignment in a clear way.

CHAPTER SUMMARY

This chapter has focused on some important skills in academic writing; presenting, evaluating, making judgements on concepts and data. The examples and activities provided have given you the opportunity to try out these skills in a step-by-step way. We have also considered some pitfalls in academic writing and ways of avoiding them. You will need to continue to practise and develop these skills in order to successfully progress in your studies. Without basic competence in the ability to organise your thinking and present it clearly, it will be difficult to achieve what will be required of you at the next level of the degree.

Hopkins, G (1998a) *Plain English for social services: A guide to better communication*. Lyme Regis: Russell House Publishing.

Hopkins, G (1998b) *The write stuff: A guide to effective writing in social care and related services*. Lyme Regis: Russell House Publishing.
These books present, in a light-hearted way, serious arguments about the importance of clear writing in social work practice. The points Hopkins makes very clearly are also relevant to social work students.

Cottrell, S (2004) *The study skills handbook*. 2nd edition. Basingstoke: Palgrave.

Northedge, A (2005) *The good study guide*. 2nd edition. Buckingham: Open University Press.

Peck, J and Coyle, M (2005) *Write it right: a handbook for students*. Basingstoke: Palgrave.
These are useful study skills guides. Stella Cottrell's book is especially helpful and detailed. These books are written for all students so will not specifically focus on the social work degree.

Part Two

Chapter 5

Developing critical analysis and understanding

This chapter will help you to meet the following National Occupational Standards.

Key Role 1: Prepare for, and work with, individuals, families, carers, groups and communities to assess their needs and circumstances.

- Assess needs and options to recommend a course of action.

Key Role 2: Plan, carry out, review and evaluate social work practice, with individuals, families, carers, groups, communities and other professionals.

- Work with groups to promote individual growth, development and independence.

Key Role 6: Demonstrate professional competence in social work practice.

- Work within agreed standards of social work practice and ensure own professional development.
- Research, analyse and use current knowledge of best social work practice.

It will introduce you to the following academic standards set out in the social work subject benchmark statement.

5.1 During their degree studies in social work, honours graduates should acquire, critically evaluate, apply and integrate knowledge and understanding in the following five core areas of study.

5.1.1 Social work services, service users and carers.

5.1.2 The service delivery context.

5.1.3 Values and ethics.

5.1.4 Social work theory.

5.1.5 The nature of social work practice.

5.2 Honours graduates in social work should be able to plan problem-solving activities, ie to:

- Think logically, systematically and reflectively.

5.3 Honours graduates in social work should be able to analyse and synthesise knowledge gained for problem-solving purposes, i.e. to:

- analyse information gathered, weighing competing evidence and modifying their viewpoint in light of new information then relate this information to a particular task, situation or problem;
- assess the merits of contrasting theories, explanations, research, policies and procedures.

It will help you meet the Quality Assurance Agency for Higher Education (2001) requirement that students studying at Level 2 (I level) are able to demonstrate:

i. knowledge and critical understanding of the well-established principles of their area(s) of study and of the ways in which those principles have developed.

and

a. use a range of established techniques to initiate and undertake critical analysis of information and to propose solutions to problems arising from that analysis;

b. effectively communicate information, and arguments and analysis, in a variety of forms, to specialist and non-specialist audiences and deploy key techniques of the discipline effectively.

Introduction

At this intermediate (I) level of the degree, undergraduate students are expected to be able to use critical thinking to understand their subject, to analyse issues and to propose solutions. In addition they should be able to communicate all this effectively. During the rest of your degree studies you will be expected to continue to develop and enhance your ability to think critically in order to explore issues of greater complexity. In this chapter we will explore what is meant by critical thinking in the academic world; the challenges it poses; the stages of development; and how to develop this aptitude.

After reading this chapter you should be able to:

- appreciate what is meant by critical thinking;

- know what is required to think and write in a critically analytic way;

- apply critical analysis to a social work issue.

What is critical thinking?

The outline below combines and synthesises some ideas about the ingredients of critical thinking.

RESEARCH SUMMARY

Critical thinking involves the following.

- *Taking a questioning and sceptical stance.*

- *Aiming for a deep understanding of knowledge and complex ideas. This includes an appreciation of the context of the ideas; their history; their construction; their relationship to other knowledge. This means not seeing knowledge as a series of facts.*

- *Exploring a range of alternative ideas.*

- *Identifying and challenging the assumptions that underlie ideas.*

- *Examining the evidence for knowledge and ideas.*

- *Recognising the role of feelings when working with ideas.*

- *Being able to use ideas and to make an argument and an informed judgement.*

- *Taking a critical stance towards your own process of thinking. This is one aspect of metacognition which we will deal with in more depth in Chapter 10.*

(Barnett, 1994; Cottrell, 2005; Moon, 2005; Redmond, 2006)

You will find that the term 'analysis' is often combined with 'critical'. Below is a definition of analysis.

Analysis involves:

- examining in detail the different aspects of an issue;

- looking at something from different perspectives;

- breaking something into its component parts.

You will see that there is some overlap between the two – both involve looking at an issue in depth and detail; both require you to use different perspectives to consider an issue. Analysis also involves breaking something into its elements or constituent parts. When thinking critically, analytic skills will be necessary; however, because critical thinking includes many more thought processes, you need to go beyond analysis.

CASE STUDY

Analysing a video clip

On Dan's course the students were shown a short video clip of a social worker, Jean, visiting an older man, Eric, in a residential home where he was living temporarily while his house was cleared of an infestation of moths. After watching the video the students were asked to work in groups to write an analysis of the interaction between Jean and Eric.

One group wrote a short description of what had happened.

> Jean introduced herself and tried to get Eric to sign some papers. Eric became angry and Jean offered to leave. Eric had told her to go.

One group formed a judgement, not based on evidence, and wrote the following.

> Jean was insensitive to Eric and he was a difficult man so the interaction was never going to work.

The tutor encouraged the group to be more analytic. She asked them to consider the following.

- *The verbal communication used by Jean and Eric; the words and expressions used and the explicit and implicit messages conveyed by them.*

- *The pace of the interaction.*

CASE STUDY continued

- *The non-verbal communication – the body language, the expressions on their faces, where Jean sat.*

- *What it might have felt like to be Jean in that situation – what was she trying to achieve?*

- *What it might have felt like to be Eric? Why might be have seemed to be unco-operative?*

- *The four phases of the interaction: the introduction; the focus on the task; the argument; and Jean's exit. What happened in each phase? What could have been done differently? Could Jean have rescued the situation?*

By using these questions the tutor encouraged the students to break the interaction between Eric and Jean into its component parts and hence be more analytical. This enabled the students to think much more carefully and to identify how it could have been handled differently. The tutor asked the students to read about communication (Koprowska, 2005, Chapters 1 and 2) before the next session so that this analysis could be linked to theories.

Developing as a critical thinker

ACTIVITY **5.1**

Areas for development

Read the above list of aspects of critical thinking carefully. Then write down the ways in which your thinking will need to develop in order for you to become a critical thinker.

Comment
Below you will find some ways of developing critical thinking illustrated with some case studies of students.

Knowing when critical thinking is needed

It will be important to appreciate when assignment titles and marking criteria are specifically requiring critical thought. When this is the case you will usually find the adjective 'critically' in front of a verb, for example:

- critically analyse

- critically investigate

- critically evaluate

- critically explore.

However, at Levels I and H of the degree critical thinking is routinely expected. It should be an integral part of the way you think and approach your studies – not just when it is included in the assignment or essay title.

Taking a different approach to learning

You will need to develop a deep rather than surface approach to learning (Moon, 2005). Thompson (2002) notes that an important part of critical thinking is not being reductionist – students must explore the complexity and many sides of an issue rather then reducing it to a single explanation. Taking a deep approach to learning will enable you to avoid taking issues at face value and help you to identify and challenge the, often hidden, assumptions behind arguments. In Chapter 1 we considered deep, surface and strategic approaches and noted their characteristics. We also noted that they are not fixed and that students can develop approaches which are more conducive to learning (Entwistle et al., 2001).

Understanding the academic use of 'critical'

In the academic world, taking a critical stance does not carry the negative meaning that some people might assume.

CASE STUDY

Nicola seeking clarification

When she saw the term 'criticise' in an assignment guideline, Nicola felt uncomfortable. She thought being critical meant making a negative comment – and her mother had taught her that being critical was rude. Similarly when she saw the term 'argument' she was uneasy. She often pulled her children up for arguing and bickering. In a tutorial she asked what these terms meant and her tutor explained their academic use. He clarified that in the academic world to be critical is acceptable. It does not mean being harsh or unpleasant but instead it is about the careful examination of ideas in order to put together a reasoned and well thought-out piece of work.

Making an argument is not necessarily about disagreement but involves using reasons and evidence to support a particular point of view. After thinking about this explanation Nicola felt relieved; it gave her confidence to begin to question what she was reading.

Becoming an active learner

You will need to develop your capacity to become an active learner. In critical thinking you are learning to learn as well as learning about social work. However, students sometimes start with what Freire (1972) called the 'banking' concept of learning. They envisage that knowledgeable, powerful, tutors will fill them up with what they need to know, providing the answers to all their questions. This view is sometimes held because of students' experiences of school where they were expected to be passive learners. If this has been the case it can be a struggle to move to becoming an active learner who is discovering things for themself and creating new ideas.

> **CASE STUDY**
>
> ### *Dan and the banking model*
>
> *Dan tended to adopt the banking model of learning. He was so keen to get his qualification that he wanted tutors to tell him what he needed to know so he could get on with things. Being on the course became quite difficult for him but he did not want to give up. He decided to go and see the training officer, Liz Burns, who had encouraged him in his ambition to achieve a professional qualification. Liz gave Dan some space to talk about his feelings of annoyance and frustration. Then she suggested to him that it might be helpful to do some learning about learning. Together they identified some of the learning activities Dan could work on: slowing down; reflecting; exploring assumptions; trying to think of alternative ways of thinking; looking out for connections between his knowledge and new material. Dan did not find this easy but because of his strong motivation to be a professional social worker he persevered with it.*
>
> *Critical thinking is a deeper, more complex way of thinking. It is one of the key differences between Level C and Level I. Like Dan you may need to examine yourself and go through some struggles in order to move to a more active way of learning.*

Nervousness about making judgements

Students can be anxious about their ability, or even their right, to make judgements about theories and ideas.

> **CASE STUDY**
>
> ### *Saranita finding out about making judgements*
>
> *Saranita found this part of the work on the course particularly difficult. She could not see how it would be acceptable for her, a 19-year-old young woman with not much experience of the world, to comment on the writing of great thinkers who had published books. On her A-level course she had enjoyed finding things out and learning what other people thought. What was required on her social work degree was very different. She discussed this with her tutor, Penny, who explained to her that it was an accepted part of being an academic thinker and writer that your ideas would be challenged, critiqued, explored and developed. She clarified that, in academic work, making a judgement was not a negative comment on someone's work but rather a reasoned conclusion based on weighing up positives and negatives. She reminded Saranita of the social work textbook she, Penny, had written about working with older people. It had been very interesting, Penny said, that students had valued some parts of the book, and critiqued other sections which insufficiently focused on the reality of everyday practice. When a second edition of the book had been commissioned Penny had revised some of the work in line with the student comments.*

Seeing the relevance to social work practice

Some students might find it difficult to see the relevance of critical thinking for a degree in social work, which is about getting on and doing things – not deep thinking. However, as discussed before, these thinking skills are transferable to the practice of social work. Practitioners are required, on a daily basis, to make decisions about complex issues, most of which will not have a single correct answer. Social workers must be able to consider the possible options based on an analysis of the impact of different approaches. They need to weigh evidence, examine arguments and understand and demonstrate the thinking and reasoning underlying their decisions. Critical thinking will help them do this and is the basis and foundation of thoughtful resolution of issues and effective practice. Moon (2005) notes that students on placements have a real opportunity to use their critical thinking skills through making judgments and decisions about live issues. This is why, on your course, as well as using these skills to consider theories and approaches, you may be asked to critically analyse case studies or incidents from practice.

In Chapter 7 we will be considering reflective thinking and practice. Here it is worth noting that there is a strong link between reflective thinking and critical thinking. While reflection tends to be more about one's own self, experiences and feelings, reflective activities can support critical thinking.

The stages in critical thinking

It can be helpful when considering a complex process such as critical thinking to separate it into stages. Again I have synthesised ideas from writers on the subject.

Critical thinking includes identifying a range of positions, arguments and conclusions; evaluating the evidence for alternative points of view and weighing up opposing arguments. We began to do this in a descriptive way in Chapter 4 when considering Nicola's assignment and the essay on advocacy. However, critical thinking is broader and deeper. In particular it extends and amplifies the ways in which students should evaluate ideas. This includes the following aspects.

- Exploring the history of the ideas and principles under consideration.

- Reading between the lines, identifying the assumptions and value positions behind the thinking. In social work this could mean utilising professional values.

- Developing a sound understanding of the sources of evidence for the ideas and evaluating them: appreciating the difference between primary and secondary sources.

- Thinking about the limitations of the ideas. Searching for flaws and weaknesses in the arguments. This requires a realisation and understanding that all knowledge is contested, challengeable and open to debate.

- Reflecting on issues in a structured way; thinking about why, emotionally, some ideas might be more appealing than others and why.

- Making judgements and drawing conclusions, based on all of the above, about the validity of the idea, using the best evidence.

- Putting forward your own proposition, while recognising its limited nature, in a structured, clear and well reasoned way.

(Barnett, 1994; Cottrell, 2005; Moon, 2005).

Using critical thinking

ACTIVITY **5.2**

An essay which requires critical thinking

Below is an example of an assignment in which you are required to demonstrate critical thinking.

Understanding domestic violence is an essential component of good social work practice. Critically discuss.

In order to develop your ability to critical analyse, first consider and record what you might need to cover under each aspect of critical thinking listed above.

Comment

Below are some comments, under each of the above stages, to illustrate how they could be used to assist your critical thinking in working on this assignment. The length of your answer will be dictated by the required word count. However, it will assist your development as a critical thinker to aim for breadth and depth in your exploration of sources and ideas.

Identifying a range of positions, arguments and conclusions

This means you would need to identify several different perspectives on domestic violence and its significance in social work practice. In order to do this you should explore a range of positions on the definition, causes and impact of domestic violence. You would need to use standard textbooks dealing with theories from sociology and psychology as well as material covering legal and social policy perspectives. Part of your exploration would be an examination of the evidence supporting different arguments. This might require you to consider research articles, current and historical statistics on domestic violence together with policy documents. Some specialist websites might also be useful sources.

In your search of relevant literature you should give consideration to groups who have traditionally been marginalised – for example, people from black and minority ethnic communities, older and disabled people. However, because the question asks you to think about domestic violence and social work you would also explore texts to uncover views on the importance of domestic violence in social work practice. This search might reveal gaps – for example, social work books which do not discuss domestic violence or a lack of literature concerning disabled people. Sometimes what is not mentioned can be as important as what is – in this instance it could give an indication of social work settings where domestic violence is not viewed as significant.

Exploring the history of the ideas and principles under consideration

Here you would be exploring how ideas about domestic violence, including its significance for social work practice, have developed historically. This could include:

- the lack of public attention before the 1970s;

- the factors in development of understanding in the 1970s;

- current definitions;

- historical and current theories on causes;

- statistics on its extent;

- social work's historical and current response to domestic violence.

Implicit in this would be researching the history of social work ideas, how these have evolved and shifted and some explanations for this. Using this approach to considering domestic violence should help you grasp the understanding that knowledge is not absolute; it is constructed; it shifts and changes. Some of the ways this has happened should be apparent from your exploration.

Reading between the lines, identifying the assumptions and value positions behind the thinking. In social work this could mean utilising the values of the profession

Here you would be expected to consider the values reflected in different understandings of domestic violence. This might incorporate:

- the values implicit in the use of the term 'domestic violence';

- the assumptions which lie behind the view that domestic violence is a private matter to be sorted out within the family;

- the feminist writers of the 1970s and 1980s who rejected traditional individualistic explanations of domestic violence and instead focused on theories of patriarchy;

- the values which underlie social work's current concern with the impact of domestic violence on children.

Developing a sound understanding of the sources of evidence for the ideas. Evaluating the sources of evidence: appreciating the difference between primary and secondary sources

When examining different sides of an argument you need to know where to find the evidence that might either support or dispute that position. This will include accessing valid and relevant sources of material as discussed earlier. To achieve this you should have a good appreciation of the range of sources available and be able to select appropriately. While your course handbooks will include reading lists, you may need to delve deeper and it can be particularly helpful to examine the references upon which the authors you are reading have drawn.

Primary, or original, sources are those produced or published at the time of the events under consideration. For this assignment these might be:

- books from the 1970s which were written to convey the emerging feminist analysis of domestic violence;
- contemporary accounts of people's experience of how social workers responded to domestic violence;
- social work textbooks written several decades ago;
- the data from research on domestic violence and social work;
- policy documents from relevant periods.

Secondary sources are materials written or produced about the issue, usually some time later. For this assignment these might be:

- books, articles, web pages about domestic violence;
- reports of research studies on domestic violence and social work;
- current documents about the setting up of the first women's refuges.

At this stage of your studies you will probably tend to use mostly secondary sources. However, some books, known as seminal texts, provided such new and original thinking that they continue to play an important role in the understanding of the subject. It can be helpful to take the time to read them rather than relying on secondary sources.

An example for this assignment would be:

Dobash, R and Dobash, R (1980) *Violence against wives: A case against the patriarchy*. Shepton Mallet: Open Books.

This book is an account of research of violence towards wives carried out in Scotland in the 1970s. Based on their research, Dobash and Dobash argue that the patriarchal family system where the husband's authority creates a subordinate position for women is fundamental to understanding violence to wives. They found that many incidents of abuse arose from arguments about money, housework or childcare and men asserted their authority and power through the use of violence.

Evaluating the sources will also mean considering the usefulness of the source of evidence. You could ask:

- what is its relevance?
- does it provide a useful theoretical perspective?
- does this help me to open up the debate or does it close it down?
- was this an important contribution to changing the way domestic violence was understood?

Thinking about the limitations of the ideas. Searching for flaws and weaknesses in the arguments. This requires a realisation and understanding that all knowledge is contested, challengeable and open to debate

Exploring the history and range of ideas about domestic violence and social work should have demonstrated that there have been, and still are, different views. However, it is not sufficient to grasp the ideas; recognising that all knowledge must be open to scrutiny, you will also need to explore their limitations. The list, suggested for evaluating, set out in Chapter 4 could be used here.

- What were the strengths?

- Why are these strengths?

- What were the weaknesses?

- Why are these weaknesses?

- What was not covered; what gaps are there?

- What aspects of social justice were considered?

- What aspects of social justice were not taken into account?

- Were the values of social work integrated?

Reflecting on issues in a structured way; thinking about why emotionally some ideas might be more appealing than others and why

Here you should think about how your own experiences, or lack of personal knowledge, of domestic violence might leave you more sympathetic to one view rather than another. For example, you might feel very drawn to research evidence that suggests that social workers are unsympathetic to mothers experiencing domestic violence. Your reasons for this could be based on sympathy towards a friend who told you that a duty social worker was dismissive of her when she explained her situation. But you might experience resistance to some arguments because they remind you of some issues which you had not previously considered. This might cause you some discomfort about your social work practice. For example, in exploring a definition of domestic violence you may have developed a new awareness that it could include older people who have been abused by their partners. This might cause you to think again about situations which you had accepted as how couples had always lived their lives, but which you now redefine as abusive. It will be important to consider and articulate why some ideas and theories are more attractive to you than others.

Making judgements and drawing conclusions, based on all of the above, about the validity of the idea, using the best evidence

At this stage you will need to systematically pull together all the ideas which you have previously explored, their strengths and their weaknesses. Your judgements about these will lead to your conclusions. In this assignment you will need to keep the focus on the statement

Understanding domestic violence is an essential component of good social work practice
So you will need to conclude whether this statement is valid and give your reasons for your assertion. Having examined all the evidence you might, for example, conclude that for good social work practice having an understanding of domestic violence is necessary, but not sufficient, because understanding does not seem to lead to changes in the way social workers work with families.

Putting forward your own proposition, while recognising its limited nature, in a structured, clear and well reasoned way

Finally, as a critical thinker, following on from your conclusions you should be able to put forward your own thoughts on the issue. In this example you might include thinking about ways in which social workers' understanding might be translated into action. So your proposition might be that:

• social workers should challenge each other's practice;

• team managers should raise issues of practice on domestic violence in supervision.

Your proposals should relate back to, and follow logically from, the arguments made in the assignment.

In this example we have not considered how you might structure your assignment. The purpose has been to provide you with an experience of what it might mean to put into practice some of the aspects of critical thinking.

The characteristics of critical thinkers

ACTIVITY **5.3**

Critical thinkers

Given what you have now learnt about critical thinking, make a list of the attributes of student social workers who are critical thinkers.

Comment

You might have come up with some of the following:

• an enquiring and curious mind;

• intellectual honesty;

• well read with a good background knowledge of social work in its broad context;

• open-mindedness;

• intelligent scepticism or polite doubt – in the the Victoria Climbié Inquiry Lord Laming (2003:6, p602) called this *respectful uncertainty*;

• the ability to think in a systematic way;

• the ability to identify the argument among other types of writing;

• self-knowledge – being aware why we might prefer one explanation to another;

• open to challenge: ready to have long-held assumptions challenged;

• being prepared to move beyond the comfort zone of what you know;

• brave enough to take some risks;

- the capacity to use support to develop the confidence necessary for forming your own viewpoint.

(Barnett, 1994; Coleman et al., 2002; Cottrell, 2005; Moon, 2005)

ACTIVITY 5.4

Self-evaluation

Take some time to consider which of the above attributes of a critically thinking social work student you possess and which you need to develop.

Comment

This is, of course, a formidable list – one to aim for, not where you would expect to be at this stage. It is worth noting that the list includes affective or emotional qualities in addition to cognitive or thinking attributes.

Using critical thinking to explore a situation from practice

During your course you will be expected to apply your critical thinking and analysis skills to case studies or incidents from practice. This would entail using the theories, knowledge and understanding you have developed as tools to make sense of a situation and inform your social work.

CASE STUDY

James Mills

James Mills (2 years 5 months) is looked after by his maternal grandmother, Doreen, under kinship care arrangements. His mother is in a residential rehabilitation centre to deal with alcohol dependence. When you as the designated social worker visit you are concerned by a number of issues. James is very passive and does not seem to interact with his grandmother; he apparently has a poor appetite and does not sleep through the night. The home is sparsely furnished and Doreen tells you she is struggling financially.

ACTIVITY 5.5

Using theories to analyse

List the theories and research you would draw on to help you analyse the situation.

Comment

You might have identified the following.

- To analyse kinship care – theories of identity, sociology of the family and attachment.

- To appreciate the concerns about James – theories of child development and attachment.

- To think about the family's situation – research about the impact of living in poverty and social exclusion.

You would need to approach each of these areas of knowledge and theories from a critical perspective using the approaches described in this chapter.

Critical writing skills

Using critical writing skills should assist you in conveying your thoughts and ideas. Critical writing should:

- contain only essential descriptive writing;

- be clear and precise;

- present arguments in a consistent way;

- indicate the relevance of the material included;

- be carefully selective about the amount of detail required;

- give reasons for the selection of information;

- show how ideas or arguments are connected;

- structure information in order of importance;

- show how different arguments or ideas are connected;

- use language effectively to convey arguments and ideas;

- signpost the reader through the argument by skilful use of language;

- make a reasoned judgement;

- reach a logical conclusion based on arguments.

(Cottrell, 2005; Moon, 2005)

ACTIVITY **5.6**

Different kinds of writing

Compare this list with the outline of descriptive language in Chapter 4. Identify the differences between the two types of language.

C H A P T E R   S U M M A R Y

In this chapter we have identified what being a critical thinker means and the important characteristics and ways of developing these attributes. We have looked at two possible ways this thinking might be used in college assignments and noted the features of critical writing. It is not possible to become a critical thinker and writer simply by reading this chapter. It will be part of a process of your development as a learner, both in college and when on placement. By the end of the course you should be demonstrating these skills as you will require them both in your studies and when you become a professional social worker. This links us to the next chapter in which we explore how you can use your college learning during your practice placement.

FURTHER READING

Cottrell, S (2005) *Critical thinking skills*. Basingstoke: Palgrave Macmillan.
A comprehensive guide to developing effective analysis and argument, written for a general audience, which contains many useful activities.

Chapter 6

Applying college learning on your placement

This chapter will help you to meet the following National Occupational Standards.
Key Role 1: Prepare for, and work with, individuals, families, carers, groups and communities to assess their needs and circumstances.
- Prepare for social work contact.
- Work with individuals, families, carers, groups and communities to help them make informed decisions.
- Assess needs and options to recommend a course of action.
Key Role 2: Plan, carry out, review and evaluate social work practice with individuals, families, carers, groups, communities and other professionals.
- Interact with individuals, families, carers, groups and communities to achieve change and development and to improve life opportunities.
Key Role 6: Demonstrate professional competence in social work practice.
- Research, analyse and use current knowledge of best social work practice.

It will introduce you to the following academic standards set out in the social work subject benchmark statement:
5.1 During their degree studies in social work, honours graduates should acquire, critically evaluate, apply and integrate knowledge and understanding in the following:
5.1.1 Social work services, service users and carers.
5.1.2 The service delivery context.
5.1.3 Values and ethics.
5.1.4 Social work theory.
5.1.5 The nature of social work practice.
5.1 Honours graduates in social work should be able to plan problem-solving activities, i.e. to:
- apply ethical principles and practices critically in planning problem-solving activities.
- plan a sequence of actions to achieve specified objectives making use of research theory and other forms of evidence.
- manage processes of change drawing on research, theory and other forms of evidence.
5.3 Honours graduates in social work should be able to analyse and synthesise knowledge gained for problem-solving purposes, i.e. to:
- assess human situations, taking into account a variety of factors (including the view of participants, theoretical concept, research evidence, legislation and organisational policies and procedures).
- consider specific factors relevant to social work practice.
- assess the merits of contrasting theories, explanations, research, policies and procedures.
5.4 Honours graduates in social work should be able to use their knowledge of a range of interventions and evaluations processes selectively to:
- plan, implement and critically review processes and outcomes.

It will help you meet the Quality Assurance Agency for Higher Education (2001) requirement that students studying at Level 2 (I level) are able to demonstrate:
i. ability to apply underlying concepts and principles outside the context in which they were first studied, including, where appropriate, the applications of those principles in an employment context.

Introduction

We have previously acknowledged the applied nature of social work knowledge and the importance of making connections between college learning and social work issues. At this level of the degree in social work you are expected to be able to use what you have learnt in college in a different context, including in employment. For social work students this means applying theories and principles when you are on your practice placement, in a social work agency. The purpose of this chapter is to help you to be able to make these connections between theoretical knowledge learnt in college and the world of social work practice.

After reading this chapter you should be able to:

- see the links between your college learning and your experiences during practice learning;

- apply theories of the client world to people who use services;

- apply theories of how to do social work to your practice.

The experience of being on placement

About half of your degree course will be spent undertaking practice learning in a social work or social welfare agency. Some students relish this opportunity to 'get into the real world' and be 'hands on' after having spent some time in college. It may be tempting to see the two aspects of learning – college and practice – as separate. But it is essential that you appreciate the connection between the two and develop the ability to think about one in relation to the other. Some aspects of being on placement might work against this way of thinking. For example, students often find the beginning of a placement somewhat overwhelming.

CASE STUDY

Nicola's first placement

Nicola had really been looking forward to her placement in a Youth Offending Team (YOT). She had attended the preparation for practice learning session; looked through the college Practice Learning Handbook; bought some smart outfits in case she needed to attend court; and done background reading on the YOT. However, nothing could really have prepared her for the first few weeks of her placement. There was so much to take in – all at once. She had to find her way around a new building and the court; learn people's names and their roles in the team; understand the recording and IT systems; appreciate the culture of the organisation together with its policies and procedures; grasp the dynamics of the team; and discover how the tea fund worked. Her prior reading helped but her first impressions and observations of the work of the YOT puzzled her and, until she got to know them, she was anxious about the young offenders. Nicola was keen to learn how to practise with confidence but very self-conscious about whether she would be good enough. For the first few weeks of the placement these anxieties took up all her energy, not leaving much space in her head for college learning.

ACTIVITY **6.1**

Being on placement

Think about your experience of practice learning and identify any difficulties you faced relating college work to placement experiences.

Comment

Several factors can militate against the application of theories, concepts and principles. Using knowledge acquired when in college to work on case studies is valuable, providing a safe space to test out ideas and learn from errors. But it can seem a world away from the reality of practice where students experience the pressure of needing to provide answers, to make decisions and to perform effectively. The pace of activity on placement may suggest that there simply is not enough time to give attention to high-level thought – it being more important to get on and do the work. We noted in Chapter 3 the tendency for experienced social workers not to discuss the theories and knowledge which inform their practice. Students also face the demands of learning to become a social worker when under the spotlight of being assessed on their competence in practice. They may feel that getting on with completing their practice learning portfolio is the priority.

However, you will find that providing the evidence of your competence cannot be separated from your use of theoretical knowledge. In order to meet a satisfactory level of competence, the thinking behind your actions must be articulated. Bringing together practice and theory may be hard work. However, your goal, by the end of your degree, should be what Secker (1993) called a 'fluent approach' to practice. This means being able to choose and apply relevant knowledge and combine smoothly different sources of understanding from both theory and personal and professional experience.

Applying knowledge

To apply knowledge means to be able to put it into operation in order to help you to organise and make sense of your experiences. You should be able to use what you have learnt in college to enhance your learning during your placement. Macaulay (2000) describes it as the transfer of learning which occurs whenever existing knowledge, abilities and skills – what you already know and can do – affect the learning or performance of new tasks, or understanding and practising in a new situation. This will necessitate questioning and thinking critically (Carr, 1995). At this level of an undergraduate degree it means having *understanding of the need to select principles and facts appropriate to the problem in hand* and being able *to apply the principles* (Lyons and Bennett, 2001, p180). For social work this means using relevant knowledge to guide practice. Educational theorists approach the process slightly differently. Eraut (1994) differentiates between different kinds of professional knowledge: propositional and process. Propositional knowledge consists of theories and concepts and principles which can be used in different ways: replication, application, interpretation or association. In this chapter we are concerned with the application of propositional knowledge which involves moving your thinking from knowing that to knowing how – or what Eraut (1994) calls process knowledge. So the application of knowledge in practice involves both seeing the connections between theory and practice and using the knowledge effectively.

Another way of looking at the application of knowledge is to consider Kolb's learning cycle, which is a model or theory about how people learn (see Figure 6.1). It suggests that from concrete experiences, such as direct practical experience on placement, learners move to abstract conceptualisation, or theories and principles, through thought and reflection. This enables theories and concepts to be applied in new situations, also known as active experimentation. The cycle then continues as this experimentation leads to new concrete experiences – and the process carries on. This model helps to understand how the application of theory to real practice experience might occur, through reflection on the experience and experimentation or trying out the concepts in relation to practice. Learning therefore is an ongoing, continuous process.

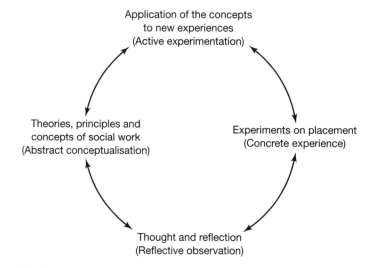

Figure 6.1 Kolb's learning cycle
Source: Adapted from Parker. J (2004) *Effective practice learning in social work*

When using the model you can either start with your experiences or with theories. If you were to begin with your placement experiences, you would apply thought and reflection to them in order to move through the cycle, to the theories and principles which might help you to make sense of them. You could then apply the theories to new situations showing how you have learned to use theory in practice. Alternatively you might start with theories and move round the cycle from there. What is important is that you will need to use and build on existing concepts. It is worth noting that simply having experiences does not lead to learning; you have to actively work with them using reflection and thought in order to develop. In this way you will be moving backwards and forwards between theory and practice (Thompson, 2002; Parker; 2004). In Chapter 7 we will consider in more detail the process of reflection, which is an important way of thinking about your experiences.

ACTIVITY **6.2**

Relating theory to practice on your placement

Think about and write down:

- *what you would find helpful from the placement to assist you in relating theory to practice;*

- *what you can do to assist the process of relating theory to practice.*

RESEARCH SUMMARY

Educational research suggests the following answers

A helpful placement will offer you:

- *the opportunity to have experiences which will support your learning;*

- *a practice assessor with whom you have a trusting relationship and who allows you to learn from your mistakes;*

- *a practice assessor who can draw your attention to the potential for transfer and help you make connections;*

- *a culture supportive to applying college learning to practice;*

- *a shared language about learning;*

- *space to think.*

You will find it easier to relate theory to practice if you are able to:

- *organise your thinking in ways that help you to recognise meaningful patterns and principles;*

- *secure a sound grasp of college learning;*

- *critically analyse;*

- *learn from experience;*

- *actively think about your experience;*

- *make a deliberate effort to relate the new experience to concepts you already possess;*

- *be a motivated learner.*

(Tennant,1999; Fisher and Somerton, 2000; Lister, 2000; Macaulay, 2000)

Writing about practice

On your course you will be required to write about your practice placement, both in your portfolio of practice learning and in college assignments. While in some academic work it is not seen as appropriate to use the first person, or 'I', in essays and assignments, in social work it is generally deemed acceptable. However, you should always check this with your tutors. In my experience the use of 'I' enables students to outline and analyse their practice more clearly in addition to explaining their thinking and reasoning.

When demonstrating your ability to apply theory to placement experiences it will be essential to keep the two components woven together in your writing. There is a risk of including a paragraph on practice followed by a paragraph on theory, but writing in this way will not show that you can make and articulate the connections. Coleman et al. (2002, p589) describe the portfolio as *the melting pot of learning*. This indicates how close the link between theory and practice should be in your thinking and writing.

Theories and practice

In Chapter 3 we noted that social work draws on theories concerning:

- the task and purpose of social work: the role of social work in society;
- practice theories: sometimes called social work approaches or method – how to go about doing social work;
- the world of service users: including the internal (psychological) world and the external (social) world.

Here we will explore an example of the application of theories of the client world before focusing on practice theories.

Theories of the external client world

Here you are asked to apply in practice theories you have learnt in college about aspects of the world of the people who use the service. On your placement you will regularly observe and experience how people live, get on with and manage their lives; what is possible for them, what is a real struggle and what is simply not within their grasp. You will learn about the services the placement agency provides; the possibilities and the limitations. You may feel very strongly about what you see – from delight and satisfaction to frustration, anger or despair. It will be important to move on from, and beyond, these observations and feelings to a conceptual and theoretical appreciation of the relevant laws and social policies which frame people's lives. You should, in your thinking, be able to move from concrete situations and people's experiences to a grasp of policies and theoretical principles underpinning them.

CASE STUDY

Using social policy

Saranita's first placement was in a housing association which provided supported living schemes for people with learning difficulties. Her practice assessor encouraged her to think in a questioning way about what she observed during the placement. Saranita kept

---

CASE STUDY *continued*

a placement diary in which she wrote about her experiences and impressions. Here are some of Saranita's observations.

> Today I visited a house, with Anna my practice assessor, to meet some of the residents and find out more about what the housing association does. We arrived about 4pm after the residents had returned from the day centre, where they had all spent the day. The house was on an ordinary street and could have been anyone's except for the small housing association sign on the front door. We had a key to get in but Anna rang the bell anyway and one of the residents answered the door. There was a support worker, Dean, on duty and he was helping someone do some cooking. The house was really quite nice; there was a lounge with a massive TV and comfy chairs; a kitchen where the four residents eat and each has their own bedroom. Also there is a sleeping-in room for the staff. The residents told me that Dean had said they were all going out ten-pin bowling that evening. I did wonder who had chosen that and if all the residents enjoyed the activity. Afterwards I asked Anna why the residents went to a day centre rather than working. She said the benefits system was really complicated and for most it wasn't worth their while looking for employment.

Most of this diary entry consists of descriptive writing outlining some aspects of Saranita's first visit. However, you can also see that she has started to think and reflect – to process – what she saw. She has wondered about the everyday lives and experiences of the residents, how decisions about activities are made and how normal the living situation is. Saranita continued to turn over these ideas and impressions in her mind. Later she looked in the *Practice Learning Handbook* and discovered she needed to write about the social, economic, and policy context of the placement. *This pushed her into thinking even harder and she began to make connections.*

Saranita was able to see the relationship between the themes in the questions she had asked herself about the lives of the residents (normality and choice) and the social policies she had studied in college. She went back to her notes, handouts and books on:

- community care including the history and closure of large institutions; the NHS and Community Care Act 1990;

- the role of pressure groups in changing policies;

- welfare rights and social policies on benefits;

- normalisation;

- the four principles of Valuing people (Department of Health 2001c) – rights, independence, choice and inclusion.

She had appropriately selected pre-existing knowledge and was able to see how her college learning related to her observations, how and why policies had changed and the profound way in which the policy context framed the lives of people with learning difficulties (Williams, 2006).

ACTIVITY 6.3

The social context of your placement

Think about the day-to-day lives and experiences of the people who use the agency where you are/have been on placement. Identify the legislation and social policies that form the context of their lives.

Comment

Shardlow (2007) suggest the following approaches to social policy are relevant to social work.

- The values or principles that might underlie social policy such as equality, social need or rights.

- The politics of social policy: for example, New Labour, the third way and modernisation.

- The content of social policy in five major areas of importance: education, health, housing, social care and social security. In turn these could be considered under the headings social issues, social problems and the experiences of groups.

It might be useful to see where your answer fits into Shardlow's approaches.

Theories of how to do social work

We will now focus on theories of how to do social work, also known as approaches or methods, and explore their application on placement. On your course you will have been taught a wide range of these from a theoretical perspective; for example, crisis intervention, task-centred, solution-focused, person-centred, group work, community work. When in college, despite using case studies and role play to become familiar with these, students often find it difficult to think about their application in practice. When you are on placement you may find it challenging to make the connections.

CASE STUDY

Using a task-centred approach

Dan's first placement was in a community-based team in a voluntary organisation providing support for vulnerable adults. After the induction period, during which he had quickly familiarised himself with the work of the team and found his feet, his practice assessor, Joan, asked him to work with a young man, Stevie Glasby. Dan was given Stevie's file to read and from this he learnt the following information.

Stevie is 20 years old and had been studying at the local college, Bellsdown University. However, in the first year of his studies he had been admitted to hospital twice, having being found unconscious after drinking very heavily. On neither occasion had he taken drugs (other than alcohol) and the psychiatrist's assessment was that he had not been attempting suicide. There was concern that he was depressed but Stevie had refused medication. Having missed a good deal of the first year of the course, Stevie had now dropped out of university but had remained in Bellsdown rather than returning to his

---

family. He was managing financially through casual kitchen work and help from his girl-friend with whom he was living.

A week ago Stevie had rung the team and asked for help; he said he felt at risk of slipping back into heavy drinking. After a team discussion it had been agreed that Dan should meet with Stevie and perhaps work with him. Joan suggested an initial meeting after which Dan should, in supervision, explain the social work approach he thought would be helpful. Dan agreed to this but privately he was anxious; he was not used to being asked to plan his work in this theory-led way. But he used his study time to refresh his memory about the range of social work approaches that had been covered in college. After the first meeting with Stevie, Dan scanned through his accumulated knowledge and decided that the task-centred approach would provide a way ahead. He observed that Stevie was very motivated to work with Dan and able to articulate his problems. The task-centred approach with its principles of collaborative problem-solving, developing people's capacity together with a focus on the 'here and now' and empowerment seemed to be positive to Dan. In supervision Joan helped Dan to think about how to apply the theory to practice – in Kolb's cycle this would be understood as active experimentation, which would lead to new experiences. At the next meeting Dan sketched out the main principles of the task-centred approach and this seemed acceptable to Stevie.

In the next and subsequent meetings Dan began to actively apply the task-centred approach, following the stages set out in the model, with Stevie. If you are not familiar with the theory you might find it helpful to refer to a social work textbook before reading on to see how Dan applied it. (You could use any of the following: Marsh and Doel, 2005; Trevithick, 2005a; Marsh, 2007; Parker and Bradley, 2007.)

1. Examination of problems

Dan asked Stevie to outline all his problems. This was the list.

Dependence on my girlfriend.

Pressure and stress from my family who want me to return home.

Tedious, boring work and no job satisfaction.

I feel a failure because of dropping out of university.

Not enough money.

Debts.

Pressure from friends I used to drink with to go out with them.

Then Dan encouraged Stevie to look in depth at the problems and to decide which one was a priority to deal with. Dan felt able to do this because there were no legal requirements preventing a service user-led view of the situation.

Stevie identified that the pressure from his family to return to the family home, 200 miles away, was the most pressing problem. He was acutely aware and guilty that he had *disappointed his parents and caused them anxiety. When he had been in hospital they had dropped everything to come and see him, when they could not really afford the train fares. However, despite his life not being as he wanted it to be, Stevie believed that he could not go back to live at home now he had achieved some independence. His parents had written and phoned and he had stopped answering the phone to them or replying to their letters because he found it all too difficult. But they still tried to get in touch with him and in their last letter said they were going to come to visit.*

2. Goal-setting

With Dan's help Stevie identified that his goal was to live in Bellsdown without feeling guilty about his parents. Stevie knew that he thought he had achieved the goal when he had clearly, positively and kindly communicated this to his mother and father.

3. Time limit

Dan and Stevie agreed to meet every week for six weeks.

4. Tasks

Dan and Stevie then together planned a series of tasks to build towards achieving the goal. These were Stevie's tasks.

Write a short note to his parents to initiate contact.

Make a five-minute telephone call to his parents to check up on how they are.

Write a letter explaining clearly his plans to stay in Bellsdown.

Follow up the letter with a telephone call conveying the same message.

These were Dan's tasks.

Give feedback on the draft of the note.

Be present when Stevie rang his parents; to time the call and to indicate to Stevie if he strayed away from the planned purpose.

Give feedback on the second letter.

Help Stevie rehearse the second phone call.

Remind Stevie of the benefits of carrying out the tasks to achieve the goal.

Each week Dan and Stevie reviewed progress. They did not find that they needed to change the tasks. By the end of the six weeks all the tasks had been achieved. Dan and Stevie evaluated the overall process. Dan was amazed by the impact of the positive achievement on Stevie, who shared with Dan his intention to set himself some new, but achievable, goals in order to make progress with his other problems. Dan had regular supervision with Joan and shared his recording with her. Through questioning and discussion she enabled him to evaluate the meetings with Stevie and plan the next step.

5. Records

Dan and Stevie kept a joint record of all of this. As tasks were achieved they ticked them off, adding to the sense of accomplishment.

After the work with Stevie was finished, Dan was able to identify a number of learning points which he thought would guide and inform him during future experiences of social work, particularly when using the task-centred approach.

One reason Dan had initially quite liked the approach was because he saw himself as a 'doing' kind of person, which seemed to fit with task-centred social work. He had to learn quickly that, in this approach, his role was to enable Stevie to find a way forward, not to do everything for him.

In Dan's view the goal that Stevie had identified was not the most important issue that needed sorting out in his life. However, because he had not identified a risk in working with Stevie's definition, he was prepared to try out the theory and see what transpired. This service user-led approach was slightly uncomfortable for Dan and he had to think carefully about this.

By the end of the six weeks Dan was much more aware of Stevie's emotional fragility and was concerned that using this approach meant he had not explored the reasons for this. Neither had Dan explored the family history or dynamics. Despite this the approach seemed to have had a positive impact. Stevie's confidence in his ability to achieve had been boosted by the success of reaching his goal.

Dan had worked hard to ensure that the process was led by Stevie. In doing so he found the person-centred approach helpful because the social worker's aim is to encourage the service user to clarify issues through non-judgemental, non-directive acceptance (Trevithick, 2005a).

ACTIVITY **6.4**

Dan's learning

Look back at the learning processes Dan went through and identify the ways in which he was able to relate theory to practice.

Comment

We can look at this in different, yet connected, ways.

- Dan was able to select, from his 'toolkit' of social work theories, an approach to use in practice by recognising the connections between the features of the approach and Stevie's situation and motivation. He ensured he had a sound understanding of task-centred working and applied it in a systematic, staged and thoughtful way. He carried out some evaluation of the usefulness of the theory.

- Dan began with propositional knowledge, what he understood about the theory of the task-centred approach, or 'knowing that'. He translated this into process knowledge or 'knowing how' the task-centred approach can work in practice.

- Using the Kolb learning cycle model Dan began with the theoretical approach which he actively applied. From this active experimentation he identified learning which he knew he would take to fresh experiences during the course.

- In all this Dan was supported by his practice assessor who used questions and discussion to support him in applying theory to practice.

It can be helpful when developing your learning skills to have an awareness of the learning process and what supports it. Appreciating how you have learnt and developed is a step towards becoming a more autonomous, self-directing student. We will discuss this further in Chapter 10.

Other applications of theory

Theories learnt in college can also help us understand dynamics, or what is unconsciously going on, between people. This could be relevant to teams and other working relationships such as supervisor/supervisee or practice assessor/student together with interactions between social workers and service users. Such issues can evoke strong feelings in people so using theory to make sense of them can be very helpful.

ACTIVITY **6.5**

Applying theory

- *Try to identify one issue in your placement which you have been puzzled by, struggled to make sense of, really enjoyed or found very interesting.*

- *Think about your 'toolkit' of knowledge.*

- *Try to identify a theory, concept or principle that you could apply to the issue, deepening your understanding of it.*

C H A P T E R   S U M M A R Y

In this chapter we have focused on how to apply learning in college to the real-life situations you may experience on placement. In order to do this we have explored some theoretical ideas about learning and begun to consider how an understanding of how we learn can help us grow and develop. However, there are some important issues to which we have given only brief attention, in particular the application of values and the importance of reflection. We turn to these in the next and later chapters.

FURTHER
READING

Parker, J (2004) *Effective practice learning in social work*. Exeter: Learning Matters.
Many important issues about undertaking practice learning are covered in this book.

Trevithick, P (2005) *Social work skills: A practice handbook*. 2nd edition. Maidenhead: Open University Press / McGraw-Hill.
This book provides useful summaries of specific social work theories.

Chapter 7

Developing as a reflective learner and practitioner

This chapter will help you to meet the following National Occupational Standards.
Key Role 5: Manage and be accountable, with supervision and support, for your own social work practice within your organisation.
- Manage and be accountable for your own work.
Key Role 6: Demonstrate professional competence in social work practice.
- Work within agreed standards of social work practice and ensure own professional development.
- Manage complex ethical issues, dilemmas and conflicts.

It will introduce you to the following academic standards set out in the social work subject benchmark statement.
5.1 Honours graduates should be able to plan problem-solving activities, i.e. to:
- think logically, systematically, critically and reflectively.
5.4 Honours graduates in social work should be able to use their knowledge of a range of interventions and evaluation processes selectively to:
- use and evaluate methods of intervention critically and reflectively.
5.5.8 Honours graduates should be able to:
- reflect on and modify their behaviour in the light of experience.

It will help you meet the Quality Assurance Agency for Higher Education (2001) requirement that students studying at Level 2 (I level) are able to demonstrate:
i. knowledge and critical understanding of the well-established principles of their area(s) of study and of the ways in which those principles have developed;
ii. ability to apply underlying concepts and principles outside the context in which they were first studied, including, where appropriate, the applications of those principles in an employment context;
iii. knowledge of the main methods of enquiry in their subject(s), and ability to evaluate critically the appropriateness of different approaches to solving problems in the field of study;
iv. an understanding of the limits of their knowledge, and how this influences analyses and interpretations based on that knowledge;
and
a. use a range of established techniques to initiate and undertake critical analysis of information, and to propose solutions to problems arising from that analysis.

Introduction

The purpose of this chapter is to introduce you to the notion of reflective thinking, an approach to learning which has gained significance in recent years, especially in social work. While it is not included in the generic benchmark statement (QAA, 2001), it could be argued that it is implicit, subsumed in the general academic requirements since thinking reflectively is now generally considered to be part of approaches to solving problems. In contrast, you will see that reflection is clearly mentioned in the specific requirements for social work graduates (QAA, 2008); it is viewed as crucial to the process of becoming a professional social worker. In this chapter we will explore reflective thinking before considering what this means for developing as a reflective social work practitioner. The next part of the book will cover the integration of reflective thinking into the repertoire of the social worker able to manage complexity.

After reading this chapter you should be able to:

- understand what is meant by reflection;

- appreciate why reflection is important in developing knowledge and understanding in social work;

- apply the principles of reflection to your own learning and practice;

- understand how to write reflectively.

What is reflective thinking?

Reflective thinking:

- is the purposeful process of consideration and reconsideration of learning material (knowledge, ideas or experiences);

- tends to occur when the learning material is complex or unpredictable;

- involves deep thinking;

- often involves emotions;

- should lead to new understandings.

(Boud et al., 1985; Moon, 2004; Knott and Scragg, 2007)

Thinking back to the previous chapter and Kolb's cycle of learning, you will recall that reflection was one stage in Kolb's cycle of learning, located between concrete experiences and abstract concepts. So, for Kolb, it is a way of thinking which assists the process of making relationships between experiences and theoretical ideas. Schön (1983), a leading writer in this field, pointed out the importance of reflection in the development of knowledge and understanding of professionals. He argued that professional expertise could not rely on the straightforward technical application of theories to problems. Rather, professional practice, especially in work with people, is more complex because it is concerned with uncertain, complex, real-life situations including value conflicts. So professional artistry, based on reflection, is needed rather then technical competence. Other writers have taken Schön's ideas and developed them (Mezirow, 1981; Boud et al., 1985).

Boud et al. (1985, p3) define reflective thinking as *those intellectual and affective activities in which individuals engage to explore their experiences in order to lead to new understanding and appreciation*. They see the important ingredients as:

- intellectual activity – thinking;

- affective activity – feeling or experiencing emotions;

- using these to explore or find out more about experiences;

- the result, which should be different and fresh thinking.

These are the features of reflective thinking.

- It builds on and develops critical thinking, adding other components.

- It requires the deep approach to learning outlined in Chapter 1 because it delves and explores beneath the surface and goes beyond a superficial understanding of issues. It includes not only our experience and practice but also how we have gone about things and the understandings that lie beneath what we have done.

- In exploring beneath the surface, reflective thinking welcomes challenge, doubt, uncertainty and contradictions.

- The professional is an active participant in the use and development of knowledge. So the individual's own experiences and feelings become resources to assist in developing understanding rather than issues that get in the way of constructing knowledge.

- It can be helped by the learner being exposed to thinking from a different angle or perspective.

- It is aided by developing understanding and self-awareness of your own learning, or metacognition, an issue we will return to in Chapter 10.

- The new understanding will have an impact on professional practice.

(Boud et al., 1985; Taylor and White, 2000; Ruch, 2002; Redmond, 2006; Knott and Spragg, 2007)

The importance of feelings in reflection

Exploring and attempting to understand one's own feelings are important aspects of reflective thinking. Sometimes reflection may be triggered by uncomfortable feelings (Gibbons and Gray, 2002). But exploration of one's feelings should also routinely be part of reflection because emotion can play an important role in influencing the way in which we experience situations and make sense of them. In reflection we need to learn to be aware of and analyse our feelings. Boud et al. (1985, p26) argue that an important aspect of reflection is *attending to feelings*. By this they mean an exploration of negative and positive feelings – both those experienced during the incident upon which you are reflecting, and those experienced during the reflection. They argue that it may be important to deal with negative feelings which obstruct a reflective consideration of events.

Reflection and social work practice

The importance of reflective thinking

Thinking about what is involved in social work practice, write down as many reasons as you can why reflective thinking might be important in social work education, training and practice.

Comment

Compare your reasons with the list below.

Reflective thinking is seen as particularly important in both social work education and training and day-to-day practice for a number of reasons.

- Social work is an activity where the reasons for the decisions made about people's lives should be thought out and articulated so that social workers can be held accountable. This is particularly relevant since decisions may be based on particular values or assumptions. Reflective thinking looks beneath the surface and explores what might be taken for granted.

- Reflective thinking can help to avoid the risk of doing social work in a routine way because it sees that each situation has unique aspects to it and these need to be explored.

- Social work is a profession in which the development of practice and learning, during and through experience, is seen as a valuable way of taking forward knowledge and understanding.

- Reflection helps us move beyond our current frameworks of thinking and opens up ideas to questioning and challenge. It enables practitioners to consider different perspectives on issues.

- Because social workers are part of the experience they are seeking to understand, and part of the way in which they intervene in people's lives, they need be able to think about the impact of their selves on situations.

- The concern in social work to develop ways of working which are anti-oppressive and empowering, and the need for practice of and feedback on these, requires practitioners to be reflective.

- Reflective thinking sees as vital an exploration of feelings and their impact on one's approach. This chimes well with social work, a profession where strong feelings about the task, the context and the people who use the services can be evoked.

- Reflective thinking can ensure that the linking of theory and practice is more than the technical applications of ideas and also involves creative and flexible thinking.

- A reflective approach fits well with the complex nature of social work in which a range of perspectives needs to be incorporated.

- Adopting a reflective approach can be one way of keeping a focus on positive social work when faced with the pressures and constraints of practice.

- Reflective thinking can contribute to an understanding of the skills the social worker is using.

(Taylor and White, 2000; Dempsey et al., 2001; Trevithick, 2005a; Harrison and Ruch, 2007;)

Reflection may be used in social work in two main ways. Reflection *in* action involves thinking things through reflectively while also taking part in them. An example might be reflection during a meeting with a service user, in a case review or while having a telephone conversation. This is a complex activity which we will explore more in Part Three. Reflection on action means thinking back on an event or piece of practice, such as those mentioned previously, and thinking through what happened in a structured and systematic way. At this stage of the course it will be important to develop the habits of reflection on action – to routinely revisit experiences and explore them reflectively.

CASE STUDY

Dan learning about reflection on action

Dan had been working with Millie Solomon for two months. Millie experienced severe depression ten years ago, for which she had spent several spells as an in-patient. She is currently living with a new partner, Sue, whom she met at the day centre. Dan is finding the weekly meetings with Millie difficult – he does not find it easy to relate to her; he finds her draining and is often inwardly irritated by the way she complains about Sue. Whenever Dan supports Millie in resolving one problem, she presents him with another. Dan shared this in supervision with his practice assessor, Joan. She suggested that he took some time to reflect on, and write about, his most recent meeting with Millie. In order to organise his thinking she suggested using the following headings.

- *What happened during the meeting?*

- *Why did you go about it in this way?*

- *What were your thoughts and feelings during the meeting?*

- *Why did you think and feel this way?*

- *How did Millie feel?*

- *What were your thoughts afterwards?*

- *What theories and knowledge did you draw on?*

- *What values did you draw on?*

- *What have you learnt?*

- *What might you do differently next time?*

In order to help Dan to open up his thinking, Joan gave him some reading about issues of sexuality and social work, covering the experiences of people who use mental health services. Before the next supervision session Dan gave Joan a copy of what he had written. During the session they had a fruitful discussion based on Dan's reflective writing. This was helpful in identifying how Dan's perceptions about lesbian sexuality and his thinking about mental health service users were challenged by working with Millie. Joan supported Dan to explore how this might be impacting on Dan's ability to work with Millie and through this he was able to approach his work with Millie differently.

Students' experiences of being asked to be reflective

The benefits of becoming reflective thinkers are clear – students develop a deeper understanding of themselves and other factors and how this insight impacts on learning and practice. However, there is some limited research which suggests that students can find it a struggle.

- *Some students initially found it surprising that they were expected to be actively reflective and that tutors did not have all the answers (Thorpe, 2000; Ruch, 2002).*

- *In Redmond's (2006) action research, the students found that the process of reflection could be really challenging. This was especially the case when students were presented with the different perspectives of service users because these involved changes and shifts in their thinking. The students used terms such as 'guilty', 'uneasy', 'thought-provoking', 'humbling' to describe their initial response to the session. But later they were able to use the experience reflectively to rethink their approach to people who use services, and their changes in turn led to new opportunities for service users to change.*

- *Ruch (2002) observes how reflection can be difficult for students because it involves a lack of certainty – when students want to be reassured by clarity and straightforward answers. However, she argues that it is important to learn to live with a level of not knowing, uncertainty and ambivalence, so that students can be prepared for the complex and messy world of social work.*

- *Other students who were engaged in reflecting on prior life and work experiences described feelings of helplessness, inadequacy and disillusionment. But by the end of the course they gave more positive feedback.*

  It was uncomfortable at times, looking back at how you did things, why you did them and what you take away from it. It has also been challenging...partly because it is new but also because it creates space to questions things – like your values, beliefs and attitudes. It above all has been a refreshing opportunity for assessment of our practice both positively and critically (which is also positive).

  Reflective learning has been an essential tool in the processing of my learning...it has been invaluable.

  (Dempsey et al., 2001, p640)

On your course you may be asked to participate in a number of learning activities designed to assist you to reflect, such as role play, simulation, reviewing videos of yourself, discussion, listening to different views including those of people who use services. The feedback from the students (above) suggests that while initially uncomfortable and challenging, it was important in developing their learning.

ACTIVITY **7.2**

Reflective learning

Think about how you have felt when asked to participate in activities in class which have been designed to help students to reflect. Try to list some reasons why you felt this way. Answering this honestly will involve you in some aspects of reflection. A reflective student will have some self-awareness of why they respond to situations in particular ways.

Useful questions to promote reflection

When working towards becoming a reflective thinker it can be helpful to go about it in a systematic way using questions to stimulate and promote your thinking.

Questions to help you think reflectively about a social work experience

Describe the experience. You could use these questions.

- What factors contributed to this experience occurring?

- What were significant background factors?

- What happened? What were the main components of the experience?

Taking the time to do this gives you the opportunity to revisit what happened in a detailed way and become aware of issues you may have forgotten or set aside as not relevant. This is the content of the experience. To really engage in reflection you need to move on to thinking about the process of the experience.

Reflect on what happened during the experience. You could use the following questions.

- What was I trying to achieve?

- Why did I go about it in the way I did?

- What knowledge/theories did I bring to the situation?

- What values did I bring to the situation?

- How did my previous experiences affect what I thought and did? Did this situation remind me of similar ones?

- What were the consequences of my actions?

- How did I feel about the experience when it was happening – both positive and negative feelings?
- Why did I feel this way?
- What was the service user's perspective on the experience; how did they think and feel?
- How do I know that this was their perspective?
- Why was this their perspective?
- Are there other people's perspectives I need to think about?
- What factors influenced my decisions and actions during the experience?

Reflective thoughts after the experience. You could use the following questions.

- What was the impact for the service user of the way I went about this?
- What was the impact on me?
- What other choices did I have?
- What might have been the consequences of the other choices?

Learning from the experience. You could use the following questions.

- How do I feel now about the experience?
- Could I have dealt with it differently?
- What theories have I drawn on to help me understand this?
- What values have I drawn on to help me understand this?
- What gaps still exist in my understanding?
- What have I learnt from this which I might be able to use in new situations?
- What might get in the way of my doing things differently?

This is a long and comprehensive list of questions to be answered which demonstrates the depth and breadth that is important in reflective thinking. You may not always need to answer all the questions; however, when you first begin reflective thinking it is worth considering all of them.

You will find that reflective accounts of your practice experiences will be useful material for your placement portfolio as they will provide evidence of both your competence in particular units from the National Occupational Standards, and also of your ability to think and analyse reflectively. You may also find that such accounts are a helpful record of the development of your learning and so could be included in your personal development plan.

Nicola and Della

On her placement in the YOT Nicola found she was feeling anxious and upset about work she had just started with a young person, Della (15 years), who had been placed on a six-month supervision order for shoplifting. Whenever she met with Della, while Nicola started off with the best of intentions, the session never worked out positively. In order to try and throw new light on this Nicola wrote a reflective account of the last meeting with Della using the questions set out above.

The experience

I met Della at a burger restaurant and we both had a milk shake. I asked Della about school, the situation at home and her interests. Her answers were very brief ('OK', 'alright', 'music – you wouldn't get it') and despite my questioning I did not really get anywhere. I tried to expand on the questions and ask them in a different way but this didn't work. So I ended up doing all the talking and went on about the importance of school if she wanted to get on in life. After about half an hour Della said she had to go home and get tea for her dad so we fixed another meeting.

Reflections on what happened

My aim was to build a better relationship with Della. I knew Della's mother had left the family a year ago and this was when Della had started shoplifting. She had told my colleague that she felt alone and let down by her mother. My theory was that her offending might be linked to her sadness and that she might be helped by having a trusting relationship with an adult. I was taking a welfare approach to youth justice and planned to use a person-centred approach (Trevithick, 2005a). This was against the advice of some team members, who observed that Della came from a family well known to the police and that she was probably making a tidy sum from selling what she had shoplifted. My aim was to promote the values of respect – treating Della as an individual, not stereotyping her because of her family. I chose the burger restaurant because I thought it was where young people like to go. I wanted to gain her trust and so had worked hard to be reliable and dependable. On Tuesday I had not changed the time of our meeting even though at the last minute my son had needed a lift to football practice – I had to ask a neighbour to do it.

I was pleased Della had turned up and maybe a bit over the top about this. But then I became very frustrated by her one-word answers to my questions. It felt as if I was doing all the work. I know that I was comparing Della to my own daughter and her friends; they are all so bright and lively – it's such a pleasure chatting with them. I was not comfortable in the burger place – I hated the smell and it was noisy. The pace of our conversation was so slow and then my mind wandered; I couldn't help thinking about my son and whether the arrangements had worked out. When Della said she needed to go I was relieved as I had run out of ideas. But I also felt a failure – I felt I hadn't made any progress because my skills weren't good enough to engage her. My theory about Della wasn't right and my colleagues would point this out.

CASE STUDY *continued*

Reflective thoughts after the experience

Now I think back, I wonder what it was like for Della. Did she want to meet at the burger restaurant? Was I trying to be too 'cool' and failing dismally? Why should she open up to me in a public place? What do I look like to Della? I wonder if she picked up unconsciously that I was comparing her to my daughter – I think I mentioned that I have a teenage daughter. What does her mother leaving really mean for Della? What is family life like for her? This whole experience has shaken my confidence about using my knowledge of teenagers.

Learning from the experience

An important thing I have learnt is that I cannot assume that what I know about teenagers and families, because of my own experience, necessarily applies to everyone. My thinking needs to be much more careful. First I need to really pay attention to the diversity of people's experiences. We were taught about this in college, and I wrote about it in an essay, but until now I don't think I have really integrated it into my understanding. If I am planning to use a person-centred approach I need to really work on all three aspects – empathy, unconditional positive regard and congruence. I don't think I did very well on any of these. Actually I am not sure how easy this will be for me but I will ask Andy, my practice assessor, to help me. Also a starting point would be to aim to work in partnership with Della. This could mean explaining to her that I could have approached things better and asking for her agreement to try things differently. All this is risky for me and my confidence, especially in this team, but if I am going to develop as a practitioner I will have to take some risks.

ACTIVITY *7.3*

Practising reflection

Think back to a recent experience. It could be from your placement but it might be an experience in college. Practise thinking and writing reflectively by using the stages and questions set out above to record and explore the experience.

Tools to promote reflection

There are many ways you can develop as a reflective thinker. On your course there will be activities and assessments focusing on reflection. Below are some other ways of learning that you could use to develop your reflectiveness.

A reflective diary

Sometimes also called a reflective log or journal, this is different from a diary of events which describes what happened. Rather, the writing in it should be focused reflection on selected issues from your college or placement experience. These might be problems that are puzzling or troubling you; issues which fascinate you and you want to understand in greater depth; or experiences that you want to explore in more detail – maybe because they went really well and you want to analyse why.

Saranita's reflective diary

In Chapter 6 we saw how Saranita was keeping a diary while on her placement, working with people with learning difficulties, and that it was mostly descriptive. Her practice assessor, Anna, suggested she begin to use her diary to aim for a more reflective style. Here is an example – an account of Saranita and a resident going to a local shop.

Today I had planned to take Nadia to the local supermarket. The purpose was to assess Nadia's living skills – could she manage to find her way there, get her shopping, use social skills, pay the bill and get back to the house? Nadia had practised all this before in small tasks. Today she was going to put all this together. I had a difficult role – both going with her and assessing her. I don't think I was aware at the time how much I wanted Nadia to succeed, although I knew I was very anxious. My stomach was in knots and my heart was beating so loud I thought everyone could hear it. We set off with Nadia walking ahead and me just behind. This felt a bit false but I knew why it was necessary. Nadia arrived safely at the supermarket; she had done so well managing the pedestrian crossing on the busy road and seemed to be really confident. I was so pleased. But then she didn't go in – she just stood outside. I couldn't believe it. Anyway, eventually I joined her and, as had been agreed before with Anna, we went in and did the shopping anyway. But Nadia had lost her confidence and I was so disappointed I think I must have conveyed this to her. She didn't really manage doing the shopping very well; I had to do a lot of prompting and organise paying at the checkout. When we got back to the house Nadia didn't want anything to do with me – she sat in the lounge with Ted. I wrote in the house logbook what had happened – the bare facts, but there was much more to it than that. The staff in the house were so good with Nadia. They reminded her of all her positive achievements. I felt I had let Nadia down.

Now I have thought it over I think I should have realised the conflict I was experiencing between the role I had as an 'assessor' of Nadia's skills and my wish for her to do well. And partly I wanted her to succeed because I had been supporting her with learning some of the smaller tasks and I thought it would reflect well on me if she could manage it all. I could have talked through my hopes and fears with Anna and this might have enabled me to manage myself much better. I have now looked again at my textbook on communication skills. Before we set off I think my paralanguage (tone of voice, body language) contradicted the words I was using and conveyed anxiety and tension to Nadia: maybe this impacted on her confidence (Koprowska, 2005). When she couldn't manage to go into the supermarket my focus drifted away from Nadia to my feelings – my disappointment. In future I need to be much more conscious of the messages I am conveying. And I have thought and read more about the role of social workers and the sometimes contradictory and, for me, confusing situation that puts us in. This means I need to develop my understanding of the range of roles social workers have and think more carefully about how I approach tasks associated with different roles (Walker and Beckett, 2003). And last but definitely not least I need to talk with Nadia. But before I do that I am going to share all this with Anna.

Process recording

This form of social work recording, once required on social work courses, seems to have fallen out of fashion. It involves writing up in great depth every detail of an interview with a service user – what they said, what you said, including body language and tone of voice. So it is different from the recording that is produced for case records. However, it can be a useful tool for reflection on an interaction as it involves careful thinking back and revisiting the experience in great depth. The process can bring back to your consciousness issues you had forgotten or put to the back of your mind.

Reflective writing or discussion after watching video/DVD footage of yourself

Courses are increasingly using video cameras to assist students in the development of their communication and interpersonal skills. Once you have overcome the embarrassment of seeing yourself on the screen, it can be very helpful to take part in reflective discussion with other students and tutors about your skills. Another way of learning from seeing yourself on film is to write a reflective self-assessment afterwards.

Using a critical friend

Your own thinking and reflection can be sharpened if they are shared with someone else. The role of a critical friend is not to agree with you but to gently feed in suggestions about how the issue could be looked at from different angles.

CASE STUDY

Nicola's critical friend

In Chapter 1 we noted how Nicola had developed a critical friendship with Mandy, another student. This had been really helpful to both women. As the course progressed they continued to work together in this way. Their first placements were very different – Nicola was in the YOT while Mandy was in a day centre for older people with dementia. In some ways this difference enabled them to avoid sympathising with each other; instead they both kept a critical edge in their regular sessions.

Supervision

During your practice learning you should receive regular supervision from a practice assessor who ensures there is space during the session for you to reflect on your placement experiences. A good supervisor can really support the development of your reflective skills.

Tutorials

Small-group or individual tutorials in college can provide you with a safe, supportive space in which to talk reflectively.

Parker (2004) and Knott and Scragg (2007) explore these and other ideas in more detail.

The qualities of reflective thinkers and practitioners

The attributes of a reflective thinker

Make a list of what you consider to be the attributes of a reflective thinker.

Comment

This list is put together from what writers on reflective thinking have suggested. Reflective practitioners have attributes that include:

- self-awareness and self-knowledge;

- an openness to self-examination;

- willingness to take risks;

- critical awareness of how we have come to see the world in a particular way;

- the ability to account for a chosen course of action;

- the ability to take into account many different ways of looking at a situation;

- the ability to synthesise – that is, integrate new learning with what has been learnt before;

- emotional intelligence – being able to develop the ability to recognise and to manage emotions in yourself and others;

- curiosity about the impact of oneself;

- motivation to develop and improve practice;

- being prepared to devote time to reflection.

(Boud et al., 1985; Fisher and Somerton, 2000; Thorpe, 2000; Dempsey et al., 2001; Gibbons and Gray; 2002; Moon, 2004).

Developing as a reflective learner

Using the above list, identify the ways in which you could develop to become a more reflective learner.

Writing reflectively

In addition to *thinking* reflectively, you will, during your course, be required to *write* reflectively. As discussed earlier, reflective writing will be expected as part of your evidence in your practice learning portfolio. You might also, within an essay or assignment, be asked to reflect on your own skills; your use of theories or social work approaches; your responses to service users, colleagues or other professionals. Reflective writing demands a different writing style from other types of academic writing.

Reflective writing:

- builds on descriptive writing;
- uses theory and knowledge but goes beyond this;
- is exploratory;
- asks questions but doesn't always have the answers;
- incorporates emotional content – explores feelings;
- brings in values – both personal and professional;
- considers different ways of looking at a situation;
- involves thinking deeply;
- demands you challenge yourself;
- can be uncomfortable.

Because reflective writing is an account of your journey of reflection, it is acceptable to write in the first person, that is using 'I'.

Students sometimes find reflective writing challenging for the following reasons.

- Having learnt how to write academically, they are then expected to write in another way.

- It is exploratory and can involve revealing aspects of yourself you might feel reticent about sharing – such as doubts, prejudices, strong feelings.

- It involves writing in the first person, which some people find uncomfortable and unfamiliar. Some women students have told me that they simply find it difficult to put themselves first. Yet this is required as this student explains – *you are asked to write about yourself **big style**. You have got to be in the centre* (Rai, 2006, p789) (original emphasis).

Some pitfalls in reflective writing

- Because in reflective writing students are encouraged to explore their feelings, values and assumptions, there can be a tendency for the assignment to include material about themselves without making any connections to theories, concepts, principles or values. The tutor reading this is likely to see it as self-indulgent exploration rather than true reflective writing because of the lack of connection with established frameworks for thinking.

- Sometime students end a piece of writing with the phrase *my reflections on this are* and then continue with writing that does not show any of the characteristics of reflection. For example: *My reflections after the event were that this interview went well and Mrs*

Jones went away happy. Hopefully you can see that while this includes the word 'reflections' it does not meet the basic criteria for reflective writing.

- An appropriate balance may not be achieved between reflection and other material. It is essential that you study with care the essay or assignment guidelines and assessment criteria so you are clear about what you are aiming to achieve in the submitted piece of work.

- Reflection might occur at the end of an assignment rather than being integrated throughout the written work. A truly reflective piece of work will interweave theory, practice, values and reflection.

C H A P T E R   S U M M A R Y

In this chapter we have explored reflective thinking and its importance in both learning about and practising social work. Our focus has been on reflection on action – reflecting after the event. It has become clear that important features of reflection are, first, the incorporation of feelings and, second, how learning can emerge from reflection. Some of the challenges of reflection have been explored including the different style of writing that will be needed. A series of questions which you can use to assist you in the reflective process have been provided together with some examples. Reflection is a key skill for social workers. However, on its own it is not sufficient: reflection needs to be blended with knowledge, theory, values, practice skills and research. In Part Three we will give more consideration to reflection, particularly reflection in action and synthesising reflection with other forms of knowledge.

FURTHER READING

Martyn, H (ed.) (2000) *Developing reflective practice*. Bristol: The Policy Press.
A helpful collection of examples of reflective writing from social workers undertaking the post-qualifying child care award. The additional analytic commentaries from academic and practitioner perspectives provide useful broader context.

Knott, C and Scragg, T (eds) (2007) *Reflective practice in social work*. Exeter: Learning Matters.
An edited collection of related chapters focusing on different aspects of the reflective practitioner.

Below are examples of readings on social work and sexuality, presenting the views and experiences of people who use mental health services, which helped Dan to look differently at his work with Millie.

Bywater, J and Jones R (2007) *Sexuality and social work*. Exeter: Learning Matters

Brown, HC (1998) *Social work and sexuality: Working with lesbians and gay men*.
Basingstoke: Macmillan.

Hopkins, G (2002) *Research into practice*. Community Care, 5–11 December.

Hurford, H (2002) *In search of normality*. Community Care, 20–26 June.

O'Hara, M (2006) Prejudice, stigma, lack of respect, bullying … Service users air their common grievances. *Society Guardian*, 18 October.

Cree, VE and Davis, A (2007) *Social work: Voices from the inside*. Abingdon: Routledge (Chapter 4).

Chapter 8

Understanding and using social work research

Introduction

Pawson et al. (2003) have defined the categories of knowledge in social work thus:

- *Organisational knowledge*, governance and regulation frameworks that shape social care.
- *Practitioner knowledge*, which is difficult to collect but, as we noted in Chapter 7, particularly important in reflection.
- *Service user and carer knowledge*, which tends to be unspoken and undervalued.
- *Research knowledge*, derived from specific studies or projects.
- *Policy community knowledge*, derived from how social care fits into the complex social, political and economic environment.

So far, we have considered theories, statistics, knowledge derived from social workers' and service users' experiences and knowledge generated through reflection. In this chapter we will focus on knowledge developed through research. Although research has been mentioned in earlier chapters, we have not explored in detail what is understood by it in academic study. In this chapter we will begin to consider the role of research in developing knowledge and guiding practice in social work. This is an area where there has been considerable debate; it is a contested topic. But it is important to appreciate the arguments in order to be able to draw on research in your learning, both in college and on placement. Furthermore, at the next stage of the degree (H level) you need to be able to use and comment on and critically evaluate research. The topic of research in this chapter is therefore developed in the next part of the book.

After reading this chapter you should be able to:

- appreciate what is meant by research in academic study;
- understand the contribution of research to developing knowledge and practice in social work;
- be aware of the debates about the role of research in social work practice.

What is social work research?

A general definition of research is provided by the *Oxford Dictionary of English* Second Edition (2003):

- *The systematic investigation into and study of material sources etc in order to establish facts and reach new conclusions.*
- *An endeavour to discover new or collate old facts etc by the scientific study of a subject or by a course of critical investigation.*

So the key aspects of research are that its purpose is to find things out, to create new knowledge and the way that this is done should be organised and structured. This may entail using existing information. In social research, which is our concern, the reasons for carrying out research can be to *find or impose a pattern, to make a decision or take some action* (Alston and Bowles, 2003, p6). So, social research is not just about finding out things for intellectual curiosity, but also in order to guide decision-making or a particular intervention.

Social work research

Make a list of:

what you think the purposes of social work research might be;

issues that research in social work might investigate.

Comment

Juliet Cheetham (2002, p415) lists the purposes of social work research as follows.

- *To illuminate the aetiology of social and personal problems, including the impact of social policies on individual citizens, families and communities.*

- *To determine the impact of social work. This must include analysis of its explicit and implicit functions, tasks and processes.*

- *To influence policy and practice.*

So she takes the view that research should:

- help us understand more about people's difficulties;

- tell us about the impact of laws and government policies on people's lives;

- inform us about the difference (or not) that social work makes to service users;

- make an impact on how social work policies and practice develop.

Shaw and Norton (2007, p7), who carried out a study of social work research in universities in the United Kingdom, concluded that the purposes of social work research may be to:

- *provide objective, impartial advice for decision making, provide public accountability;*

- *generate or enhance theory and knowledge about social problems, social policy and social work and how best to develop them;*

- *develop or improve social work intervention or practice;*

- *highlight and advance the quality of lived experience, practical wisdom, and personal and organisational learning;*

- *promote social inclusion, justice or social change.*

While there are some similarities between the two lists, Shaw and Norton's is more comprehensive and has a tighter focus on the use made of knowledge produced by research.

They see that research should contribute to decision-making, lead to improvement and take forward social justice, social inclusion and social change – be socially useful.

Shaw and Norton (2007) found that social work research tends to focus on the following.

Particular groups:

- service user groupings
- citizen, user and community populations
- professional and policy groups.

Developing understanding of particular problems or issues:

- risk, vulnerability, abuse, resilience, challenging behaviour, separation, attachment, loss, disability, trauma
- equality, diversity, poverty and social exclusion
- involvement in social work; partnership; empowerment
- informal care and carers
- good practice in social work; values and ethics
- social care services
- good practice in social care management
- issues of race, ethnicity and management
- issues of gender, sexism and gender roles
- interdisciplinary social work
- the value of cross-national research
- the development of theories
- the quality of social work research
- learning and teaching in social work.

So, it is clear that social work research is broad in its range, creating new insights into many topics and issues which you might find useful in your degree studies.

ACTIVITY *8.2*

How research might be useful

Think of an issue you have come across on your placement about which you would have welcomed some research in order to help you understand it better.

> **CASE STUDY**
>
> ### Saranita's placement
>
> *When Saranita was on her first placement working with people with learning difficulties, she was taken aback to learn that one of the residents aged 40 years had been bullied and sworn at in the street by a group of youngsters. Back at college Saranita discussed this in a tutorial; another student told her that the abuse of people with learning difficulties happened a lot. The tutor suggested the students explore the research on the subject. Saranita found reports of research studies which supported the assertion by the other student. Indeed, the likelihood of verbal abuse and bullying was high – up to 47 per cent of adults had experienced it in the previous year (Williams, 2006).*

However, while in theory social work research may seem be a helpful source of knowledge, the application of research to practice is not always a straightforward matter. As mentioned in the introduction, this is a contested issue; there have been keen debates among social work academics and others about what kind of research is valid and of use in social work. Next we will briefly explore some of these debates.

Social work research – a contested issue

The origins of social work were closely linked with early social science research into the living conditions of people in poverty. However, for many years social work did not have a strong culture of research in comparison with other professions such as education and medicine (Lyons, 2002; Corby, 2006). Instead social work thinking has tended to draw on research in other more established academic disciplines such as psychology, sociology, social policy and law. Social work-specific research developed from the 1980s onwards and is gaining in strength, although Shaw and Norton (2007) note that social work still has a relatively small research community. Along with this growth emerged a keen debate concerning the kind of knowledge social work research could produce and what might be the relationship between this knowledge and social work practice. This debate was stimulated by researchers advocating evidence-based practice (EBP) in social work – an approach also prevalent in medicine, probation and education. The chief proponents, Sheldon and McDonald (1999, p1), argued that social workers carry on practising without any EBP in particular ways regardless of their effectiveness:

> *it is perfectly possible for good-hearted, well-meaning, reasonably clever, appropriately qualified, hard-working staff, employing the most promising contemporary theories available to them, to make no difference at all to (or even on occasion worsen) the condition of those whom they seek to help.*

Rather than social work continuing in this muddled way, they argued that practice should be based on best research evidence of what works. This could be revealed through research studies characterised by reliability, validity and objectivity, together with systematic reviews of the evidence on particular issues. These reviews focus on a particular practice issue and identify relevant research studies, placing greatest importance on those which have produced reliable evidence. Controlled trials which use random samples, replicable procedures and statistically verifiable results are often seen as the 'gold standard' of such research studies. The knowledge from the studies is synthesised and databases produced which, it is argued, provides evidence upon which social workers can base their practice. In medicine this approach to research and practice is more established but has also been challenged for its narrow perspective on how practice knowledge develops in human services (Payne, 2005a, b; Corby, 2006).

These criticisms have been echoed and developed by some social work academics who argue that a narrow evidence-based approach does not fit well with the complexities of social work practice. Rather than it being a technical activity which can be determined by research evidence, social work is a moral and practical activity which involves interaction, negotiation and dialogue with people, entailing listening to and learning from others and reflection on experience. It is messy and complex, taking place in people's communities, homes, residential homes and day centres rather than clinical conditions where statistically verifiable results might be obtained. So the pure EBP approach is not appropriate (Schön,1987; Parton, 2003). Rather than objective measurement being important, other criteria such as professional judgement; a contribution to social justice; empowerment; opening up debate and looking at issues in diverse ways, matter more (Beresford and Evans, 1999; Shaw and Norton, 2007). Alternative ways of seeing the relationship between research and social work practice have been suggested: research-mindedness; being research-aware; evidence-informed practice. These all suggest that the social worker or student is:

- aware of the importance and relevance of research;

- knowledgeable about what research is available;

- alert to new research;

- open to considering the implications of the research for their practice.

(Trinder, 1996; Humphries, 2007)

Rather than social workers directly determining their social work practice by using empirical research evidence, they will consider research as an important contribution to knowledge. This means that social workers need to have skills to be able to critically appraise research so as to evaluate its validity, usefulness and application to practice. We will explore this more in the next chapter.

The critics of EBP also take a broader, and more inclusive, view of research and what constitutes research knowledge. The types of research they advocate tend to be qualitative, exploring people's experiences and the meanings of these together with understanding people in their social settings. It is more likely to be small-scale case study research. In the next section we will explore some of these approaches to research, or methodologies, followed by a discussion of research methods, together with examples. This should provide a framework for the critical evaluation of research which we will consider in the next chapter.

Approaches to research or methodologies

In order to aid clarity about social work research we will differentiate between research approaches or methodologies, and research methods. The latter are the way in which information or data are collected, while the former relate to the assumptions that are made about the knowledge that can be produced from the research. Not all research texts make this distinction but understanding the difference should be helpful later when you are evaluating research. In the previous section we considered the types of research on which a pure approach to EBP rely. Below we will focus on those currently more prevalent in social work research. While we will consider each methodology separately, you will find that one piece of research may combine several of these methodologies.

ACTIVITY 8.3

Research methodology

Find the most recent edition of the British Journal of Social Work *or the* Journal of Social Work. *Select an article which is an account of a piece of social work research and of interest to you. Read it through. Then read the next section of this chapter. When you have finished, try to identify the approaches to research or methodologies used.*

Critical research

In Part Two, Chapter 2 we considered the academic meaning of 'critical' which is also relevant to critical research. The key features we noted are that it:

- takes into account the broader social, political, economic and ideological context within which the research is occurring;

- adopts a questioning and sceptical stance;

- aims for a deep understanding of the issues being researched – looks beneath the surface;

- aims to dig out and expose hidden assumptions.

Because of the concerns of social work, much research will have a critical component to it.

Example
Garrett, Paul Michael (2002) 'No Irish need apply': social work in Britain and the history and politics of exclusionary paradigms and practices. *British Journal of Social Work*, 32 (4), 477–494.

Garrett starts from the perspective that Irish people have been excluded from policy documents concerning children and families social work. He used official records, media reports and case files from the 1950s to dig beneath the surface and explore how young, unmarried pregnant Irish women travelling to England to have their babies adopted, were viewed by welfare services. Among his discoveries were that these women were routinely labelled 'PFI' or 'pregnant from Ireland' and often repatriated while pregnant or with their babies, because they were seen as a welfare burden.

Action research

Action research is a kind of applied research; it is focused on bringing about change in a policy or practice. Often the researcher may be implementing the change as well as studying its effect or impact. It aims to produce practical knowledge and does not claim to be objective or free of bias.

Example

Hart, E and Bond, M (1995) *Action research for health and social care*. Buckingham: Open University Press (Chapter 7, Case study 3) pp123–46.

Meg Bond, a social worker attached to a GP practice, had identified recurring difficulties such as inappropriate hospital discharges, lack of access to domestic services and a poor take-up of welfare benefits. Her action in response to these issues was, together with colleagues, to set up a special interest group on the elderly (SPIGE) for older people, carers and professionals. This successfully grew and moved through several phases, becoming a group *for* the elderly as its orientation shifted. Throughout Meg Bond researched the development of the group, with a particular focus on evaluation at the end of one year.

Practitioner research

In this approach the practitioner–researcher holds a job in a particular area and is at the same time carrying out systematic enquiry which is of relevance to the job. It can have overlaps with the action research described above and is likely to be small scale. Practitioner research takes advantage of the opportunities of being on the inside of an organisation to explore issues in different way from researchers looking in from the outside. This position may also present difficulties, for instance with employers and colleagues. Sometimes students on placement may carry out small pieces of research which could be described as practitioner research.

Example 1

Brown, H (2005) Carrying out research in social work. In Adams, R et al. (eds) *Social work futures*. Basingstoke: Palgrave, pp 258-9.

Helen Brown describes two pieces of practitioner research. In the first she used her experience of, reflections on, and learning from working with gay and lesbian parents together with literature reviews to write a number of publications. The second was a piece of action research evaluating the integration of assessment and care management and the care programme approach. Both were aimed at improving the quality of practice and experience for service users.

Example 2
Ruskin College

At Ruskin College some of our students were able to carry out small-scale research during their second placements. This was made easier thanks to a small grant from the Centre for Excellence in Teaching and Learning (CETL) at Warwick University which enabled the costs of the research to be reimbursed. These were the topics covered.

- The experiences of supported living workers in a supported living scheme for adults with learning disabilities.

- Pregnant unaccompanied asylum seekers: their experiences of services and strategies for their empowerment.

- Developing consumer satisfaction surveys with people who have learning disabilities.

- Debt, poverty and the threat of homelessness.

- What messages can we draw from young women with children who have engaged with an education scheme to enable a more user-friendly service?

The findings from each of these were of real benefit to the agencies where the students spent their placements, because the learning could be used to improve understanding of important issues and to develop services. In the future it may be possible for other Ruskin College social work students placed in these agencies to continue the exploration by building on these pieces of research.

Emancipatory research

Emancipatory research focuses on the lives and experiences of diverse groups who have traditionally been marginalised and under-represented. It aims to provide a voice for people from these groups, not just by the researcher presenting their views but by them being actively involved in the planning, carrying out and writing up of the research. It has a strong connection with the aims of confronting oppression and enabling empowerment, so it fits well with the values of social work. You therefore might expect to see it used widely in social work research because of the emphasis on bringing to the forefront the individual and collective knowledge of people who use services (Oliver, 1997; Beresford and Evans, 1999; Beresford and Croft, 2000). However, truly emancipatory research is difficult to achieve. It raises questions about how the voices of marginalised groups, who more often have had research done on them, can truly be heard. Three possible models for the involvement of people who use services have been suggested:

- representation in the planning and carrying out of the research;

- collaboration between researchers and people from marginalised groups;

- people from marginalised groups leading and controlling research, selecting the topics for research, dealing with the funds and themselves becoming researchers.

Following the third model in social work research would mean a shift from the type of research mostly carried out. In Helen Brown's (2005) discussion of her mental health research she notes how control shifted from the management group to service users. By the end of the project, service users had become researchers, carrying out interviews. More attention is now being given to how research needs to change to become more democratised, participatory and user-led (Shaw and Norton, 2007; Tew et al., 2007).

Example

Godel, M (2007) Ge*t the picture: Older people's lives in rural West Oxfordshire 2004–2007*. Age Concern: Oxfordshire.

Active participation of 'the researched' was a guiding principle of this innovative project. Older volunteer researchers worked alongside a professional researcher at all stages – developing the project proposal, planning the work, negotiating the research ethics, recruitment, fieldwork, analysis, dissemination, sharing and working with decision-makers. The research report includes reflection on the implications of professional researchers giving up power in order to work alongside the volunteer researchers and observes that the process of the research, how it was carried out, was as important as its findings.

Feminist research

Feminist research covers a wide range of perspectives but in general starts from the premise that there are historic and current gender power differences which mean that more attention should be given to the voices of women and that research should promote the interests of women. Feminist research has tended to consider it important to aim for a more equal relationship between the researcher and the subjects of research. In these ways it can be seen as one type of emancipatory research.

Example

Humphreys, C and Thiara, R (2003) Mental health and domestic violence: 'I call it symptoms of abuse', *British Journal of Social Work*, 33 (2), 209–26.

Humphries and Thiara (2003) carried out research commissioned by Women's Aid Federation, England, to explore the issues women and children face when leaving a violent relationship; this covered their experience of a range of welfare provision, including outreach services. So the research is concerned with women and their accounts of the responses to the violence they had experienced. In this article the focus is on mental health and responses from the medical profession to severe emotional distress. The voices of the women are centre stage in the research.

The social work research we have identified above will tend to be small-scale, case study research rather than studies of large populations. Unlike the positivist approach we discussed earlier, none of these methodologies claims to be scientific or objective. However, they should be clear and open about their bias. Many researchers using these methodologies will include a thoughtful and reflective account of their understanding of the impact of their subjective stance within the research.

Research methods

Research methods are ways of collecting information or data for the research study. You will see from the examples below that while there is a range of methods, some are more in accord with the purposes of social work research than others.

Research methods

List the ways or methods you think might be used to collect data in social work research. Then read the next section of the chapter. When you have finished check your list against the methods outlined here.

Literature review

You will find that any accounts of research, such as those found in *British Journal of Social Work* and *Journal of Social Work*, will begin with a review of the existing literature, relevant to the topic, as an introduction to the article. Masters and doctoral research students are required to review the current literature in order to provide an overview of, and analyse, the state of knowledge so far. Literature reviews can be very useful to you as a source of references. Some articles in journals are a critical review of previously written material.

Example

Dwyer, S (2005) Older people and permanent care: Whose decision? *British Journal of Social Work*, 35 (7), 1081–92.

This article pulls together official documents and research studies to explore whether older people have a role in the decisions made about their admission to residential care, with a particular focus on power. It does not include any original research by Sandra Dwyer but nevertheless provides a useful summary and raises important issues.

Documentary research

This method uses documents (often historical) to find out more about a topic. Examples of documents which might be considered in social work research could be current or historical social work texts, policy documents, correspondence, social work files and social work journals. The information gleaned from these documents is then used in the research.

Example 1: Using existing documents

Lees, S (2002) Gender, ethnicity and vulnerability: Young women in local authority care, *British Journal of Social Work*, 32 (7), 907–22.

Sue Lees was interested to explore the experience of being looked after away from home for young women with a particular focus on race. In order to do this she analysed the records of all young women over the age of 12 who came into care between 1990 and 1999 in one local authority. Obtaining permission to access the files was not easy and neither was the information she was seeking always readily available. Her findings suggested that social workers should re-evaluate some aspects of practice.

Example 2: Using documents developed for the research study

Weinberg, A et al. (2003) What do care managers do? A study of working practices in older people's services, *British Journal of Social Work*, 33 (7), 901–19.

Weinberg et al. (2003) wanted to explore how care managers in older people's services spent their working day. They asked them to complete diary schedules during one week. The content of the diaries was then analysed to ascertain the predominant activities.

Interviews

Interviews are face-to-face encounters between a researcher/interviewer and a respondent. Some interviewers, particularly those carrying out surveys, will use a standardised questionnaire. It is more likely in social work that the interviewer will adopt a less fixed approach. This might entail a semi-structured interview based on small number of open-ended questions; the researcher may ask for elaboration by asking more specific questions. In unstructured interviews the interviewer allows the interviewee free range to give an account in their own way although the interviewer may probe for more depth and detail and seek clarification. Interviews are normally recorded. You will find that interviews are often used in social work research. Feminists have challenged the idea that interviews can be objective, arguing that the personal characteristics of the interviewer and respondent are important to the how and what of the generation of knowledge. So, objectivity is unlikely, especially in less structured interviews.

Example 1
Pugh, G (1999) *Unlocking the past*. Aldershot: Ashgate.

Gill Pugh (1999) researched the experiences of ex-Barnardo's children when, as adults, they had access to social work files that had been kept on them as children. She chose in-depth, open-ended interviews as the way to elicit people's individual perceptions and feelings.

Example 2
Dustin, D (2006) Skills and knowledge needed to practice as a care manager. *Journal of Social Work*, 6 (3), 293–313.

Donna Dustin (2006) used interviews with frontline care managers and team managers to find out what they thought were the skills and knowledge needed to practise as a care manager.

Questionnaires

Questionnaires can be a structured way of gathering either quantitative or qualitative information. They may be used in face-to-face interviews, as discussed above, or sent out by post. They are a good means of systematically gathering information. The data gained from questionnaires can be analysed using computer programs.

Example
Harper, R and Hardy, S (2000) An evaluation of motivational interviewing as a method of intervention with clients in a probation setting, *British Journal of Social Work*, 30 (3), 393–400.

The purpose of this research was to evaluate the effectiveness of motivational interviewing (MI) as an approach to aid probation officers working with offenders, who misuse drugs and alcohol. Questionnaires were sent to offenders who received MI training from their probation officers before and afterwards. Another group were also sent questionnaires – they did not receive this training. The aim was to identify whether any improvement and change were connected with the MI training. The results were analysed using a computer program. Questionnaires were also sent to the probation officers and their seniors to ascertain their attitudes towards MI. The overall conclusion was that MI was more effective than non-MI work in bringing about change in offenders who had drink or drugs problems.

Ethnographic research

Ethnographic research emerges from the observation of social situations, without disturbing it, in order to understand it more fully. It aims to capture the subtleties behind formal accounts of organisations or institutions.

Example

Hall, T (2001) Caught not taught: Ethnographic research at a young people's accommodation project. In Shaw, I and Gould, N (2001) *Qualitative research in social work*. London: Sage, pp49–59.

Tom Hall (2001) describes how he carried out research in a hostel for homeless young people. He spent time in the staff office and team meetings but mostly in unobtrusive observation of the range of hostel activities, and discusses some of the conflicts and tensions in this. He concluded that the significant work of the hostel was carried out in the everyday and conversational exchanges between staff and residents over meals and routine activities, rather than through the more formal key-work sessions.

Cohort studies

These are long-term studies of people or services over periods of years to identify changes.

Example

Schofield, G and Beek, M (2005) Risk and resilience in long-term foster care, *British Journal of Social Work*, 35 (8), 1283–1301.

Schofield and Beek (2005) wanted to explore how the needs of looked-after children could be identified and met in long-term foster families provided by the local authority. They used questionnaires and in-depth interviews between 1997 and 1999 and then again in a follow-up study in 2001–2. From this they identified three groups of children: those whose progress was good, those whose progress was uncertain and children who were in a downward spiral. This enabled them to highlight factors which had contributed to their success or otherwise in foster care.

Randomised controlled trials

These have been argued to be the 'gold standard' of research by those advocating evidence-based practice and are seen as the preferred method (Shaw and Gould, 2001). In this research two groups are compared in order to test out the effect of an intervention.

People are selected randomly for the two groups in order that other factors that might impact on the outcome are evenly distributed. This research method has been used widely in medicine but so not much in social work. However, as discussed above, there is considerable debate about its value. The use of randomised, controlled trials can also raise ethical issues – an aspect of research which will be discussed in the following chapter.

Example
McDonald, G and Turner, W (2005) An experiment in helping foster carers manage challenging behaviour, *British Journal of Social Work*, 35 (8), 1265–82.

Previous research had suggested that foster parents were ill-equipped to deal with difficult behaviour in foster children. The purpose of this study was to test whether training foster carers in cognitive behavioural methods would help them to manage challenging behaviour, leading to fewer placement breakdowns. Foster carers were randomly allocated to either a cognitive behavioural training group or a waiting list group. However, the research did not demonstrate significant differences between the two groups with regard to behavioural management skills and the frequency and severity of behavioural problems.

Useful sources of research for social work students

In order to be able to use relevant research it is helpful to be aware of useful sources. Because a good deal of research is written in a style suitable for academic journals rather than being focused on helping students to learn, it can be initially difficult to find your way into using research.

ACTIVITY **8.5**

List the sources of social work research material which you have used. Then check against the sources identified below.

Research summaries

One way of beginning is to become familiar with the range of research available and its potential usefulness by drawing on summaries.

Learning Matters books provide research summaries which can be very helpful in pulling together, in an accessible way, current knowledge. If you are exploring an issue in depth you will find it helpful to use the references contained in these summaries to delve deeper into a topic.

Community Care currently carries a regular feature, *The Evidence Base for Social Care Practice*, provided by the Social Care Institute for Excellence (SCIE). These articles include:

- a summary of the research
- messages for practitioners
- short abstracts of the relevant research
- sources of further information.

The Social Care Institute for Excellence aims to:

- improve social care services for adults and children;
- identify good practice and help to embed it in everyday social care provision;
- disseminate knowledge-based good practice guidance;
- involve service users, carers, practitioners, providers and policy-makers in advancing and promoting good practice in social care;
- enhance the skills and professionalism of social care workers through tailored, targeted and user-friendly resources.

One way it achieves this is through its electronic database, *Social Care Online* www.scie-socialcareonline.org.uk/. This is an important resource and all social work students should have received information and useful materials via their course to help them use this website and other SCIE resources effectively.

Other publications

Research summaries can also be found in other publications which have surveyed and collated relevant material. For example, in children and families services, many such publications were produced by the (then) Department of Health Children's Social Care section.

Example

Quinton, D (2004) *Supporting parents: Messages from research*. London: DfES/DoH.

This publication summarises the key findings of a series of research studies all focusing on what support parents need in bringing up their children positively. It includes summaries of each piece of research and a chapter covering common themes arising from these studies.

Example

Thoburn, J et al. (2005) *Child welfare services for minority ethnic children*. London: Jessica Kingsley.

This book is an extensive overview of the research into welfare services for black and minority ethnic children and families. So it is a particularly useful summary, for example, of issues concerning children looked after or child protection.

Journals

The most relevant journals are likely to be *Journal of Social Work, Practice, Social Work in Action* and *British Journal of Social Work*. If you are looking for research on a particular topic it is worth searching these. However, as mentioned above, the style in which the articles are written is not always very accessible. Before reading the main body of the article always read the summary or abstract and the conclusion. This will alert you to the main aspects of the article and so help decide if it is worth investing time and energy on reading it in detail.

Other journals

You may also find it helpful to use journals from areas or disciplines closely linked to social work. Examples might be *Critical Social Policy, Journal of Youth Studies, Sociology, The Sociology Review, Age and Ageing, Ageing and Society, British Journal of Social Psychology, Journal of Community and Applied Social Psychology, Child Abuse Review, Legal Action.*

Websites

Pressure groups and government departments may post current research on their websites. This may be the whole research report or a summary. Good examples would be the Joseph Rowntree Foundation, Barnardos or Age Concern.

C H A P T E R   S U M M A R Y

This chapter has been an introduction to the complex issue of research and social work. It has touched upon some important debates about what counts as knowledge in social work. So we have begun to think about how research may be relevant to practice. While we have explored the assumptions behind research knowledge and how research data are collected, other aspects need to be considered, in particular the ethics of research. In the next chapter we will again consider research and how to evaluate it for use in social work practice.

FURTHER READING

For a fuller account of the debates concerning the relationship of research to social work practice you could read the following.

Dominelli, L (2005) Social work research: Contested knowledge for practice. In Adams, R, Dominelli, L and Payne, M (eds) *Social work futures: Crossing boundaries, transforming practice.* Basingstoke: Palgrave Macmillan, pp223–36.

Doel, M and Shardlow, S (2005) *Modern social work practice: Teaching and learning in practice settings.* Aldershot: Ashgate, pp179–88.

McLaughlin, H (2007) *Understanding social work research.* London: Sage, Chapter 5.

Corby, B (2006) *Applying research in social work practice.* Maidenhead: Open University Press / McGraw-Hill. This book also usefully explores social work research relating to different service user groups such child care, mental health, older people.

For more depth and detail about research methodology and methods you might find the following useful.

Alston, M and Bowles, W (2003) *Research for social workers.* Abingdon: Routledge.

Payne, G and Payne, J (2004) *Key concepts in social research.* London: Sage.

To read in more depth about emancipatory research you could look at the following:

Tew, J et al. (2006) *Values and methodologies for social research in mental health.* London: SCIE.

Oliver, M (1997) Emancipatory research; Realistic goal or impossible dream? In Barnes, C and Mercer, G (eds) *Doing disability research.* Leeds: The Disability Press, pp15–31. This book is currently only available electronically at www.leeds.ac.uk/disability-studies.

Part Three

Chapter 9

Becoming a research-informed student

and
a. apply the methods and techniques that they have learned to review, consolidate, extend and apply their knowledge and understanding and to initiate and carry out projects;
b. critically evaluate arguments, assumptions, abstract concepts and data (that may be incomplete) to make judgements, and to frame appropriate questions to achieve a solution – or identify a range of solutions – to a problem;
c. communicate information, ideas, problems and solutions to both specialist and non-specialist audiences.

Introduction

In the previous chapter we explored some debates concerning social work research, and considered how research might inform social work practice. We then focused on the ways research is conducted and what this might indicate about the knowledge it produces. The purpose of this chapter is to provide guidance on becoming a research-informed student and practitioner. We will do this by raising awareness of the significance of ethics in social work research and considering social work research in an academically more sophisticated way, developing some of the themes already discussed. First we will explore how to critically evaluate research, recognising that research can be a contested issue, incorporating ethical issues and building on the understanding of critical analysis developed in Chapter 5. Using this approach we will consider how research can be used to inform your practice in social work.

After reading this chapter you should be able to:

* use the tools of critical analysis in relation to a piece of social work research;

* critically apply research knowledge to inform social work practice.

Critically analysing research

A reminder of critical analysis

In Chapter 5 we noted the ingredients of critical analysis. Those that are particularly relevant to critical analysis of social work research are:

* taking a questioning/sceptical stance;

* identifying and challenging assumptions;

* aiming for a deep understanding of knowledge and complex ideas, including an appreciation of how knowledge has been constructed;

* examining in detail different aspects;

* breaking something into its component parts;

* looking at something from different perspectives;

- recognising the role of self: the significance of feelings and taking a critical stance towards your own process of thinking (also linked to reflection discussed in Chapter 7);

- being able to make an informed judgement.

Just as there are debates about the nature of social work research, as discussed in the previous chapter, so the issue of what constitutes good quality research in social work is contested. Shaw and Norton (2007, pix) identify a number of questions which were raised in their major investigation *The kinds and quality of social work research in UK universities*. They ask whether social work research should:

- be judged by its *value for people and value for use?*

- adhere to strict criteria for the creation of knowledge? – what they call *epistemological and knowledge building standards;*

- contribute to directly to practice?

- contribute to theory?

- always involve people who use services/carers?

- be concerned with social justice?

They note that the view most often expressed was that *rigour-with-relevance* should be the criterion by which research could be judged for quality. That is, research in social work should both meet demanding academic standards of consistency and thoroughness and be of use to the profession.

Ethics and research

An important aspect of research that we have not yet considered, which is crucial in making a judgement about research, is the ethical base of the study. Research ethics provide a code for morally good conduct when considering both what and how research can be carried out. In social research five ethical criteria must normally be met before research can proceed. These are:

- autonomy – giving respect to people being researched including confidentiality, informed consent and privacy;

- non-maleficence – not doing any harm to the subjects of the research;

- beneficience – providing some benefit to those being researched;

- justice;

- positive contribution to knowledge – ensuring professional standards, using appropriate research design, methodology, methods and analysis, reporting results honestly, not falsifying results, being open about difficulties.

(Alston and Bowles, 2003; Becker and Bryman, 2004)

Universities, colleges, local authorities and health trusts are likely to have their own code of research ethics with which staff and students must demonstrate their compliance before being given permission to proceed with research. At Ruskin College the students who carried out small-scale research projects, mentioned in the previous chapter, were required to complete an ethical approval form which was agreed and signed by their supervisor before the research started. The headings on the form are as follows.

- Purpose of study

- Design of study

- Potential benefits and risks

- Sampling procedure

- Informed consent

- Data protection

- Confidentiality and anonymity

- Dissemination of finding.

When completing the form each student explained the implications of meeting the ethical code for their particular research.

ACTIVITY 9.1

Research ethics

Locate a copy of the Code of Ethics for Research *for your college.*

Read it through carefully. Identify the aspects which you think are of most importance to social work research.

Comment

You might have identified the following.

- Because social work research could involve people who are vulnerable, the meaning of 'informed consent' might need very careful consideration.

- Since research might lead to the sharing of sensitive information, confidentiality should be thought about in depth.

- If the research has the aim of empowerment, the design of the study should be carefully thought out to reflect its aims.

Any critical analysis of social work research must integrate an understanding of the ethics of research as outlined next.

Critical analysis of research: a framework

In your studies at H Level you will be expected to use social work research in order to develop a full and specialist understanding of a topic and to guide your thinking and practice. This will mean being able both to approach research in a critical way and to identify its strengths and weaknesses and potential for informing practice. The questions set out below, which incorporate Shaw and Norton's (2007) criteria and a consideration of research ethics, provide a framework which can be used to evaluate a piece of research.

Research topic

- Is the research well informed by the existing knowledge base?
- Has it drawn on a good range of the existing literature on the topic?
- Is the research an appropriate development of the knowledge base?
- Does the research have an emancipatory focus?

Research question(s)

- What were the questions the research set out to answer?
- Are the questions well thought out and clear?
- Is the selection of research questions adequately argued and justified?
- How was the research funded and are there any possible implications?

Research ethics

- Are the research ethics clearly set out?
- Are the research ethics consistent with social justice?
- Are there ethical considerations which have been overlooked?
- Are there ethical dilemmas which have not been explored?

The conduct of the research

- How was the research carried out?
- Is the methodology clear? Is it appropriate to the topic and the research questions?
- Is the design of the research well thought out?
- What methods were used to collect the data? Are they clear and appropriate to the topic?
- Is the way the data were analysed clear and justified?

Social justice

- Is the research consistent with values of social justice?
- Did the research have a social justice and emancipatory purpose?

- What aspects of social justice are addressed?

- What aspects of social justice are not addressed; are some relevant groups excluded?

- What was the level of involvement of people who use services and carers?

Findings

- What are the main conclusions to be drawn from the research?

- Are the claims of the implications of the findings consistent with the aims of the research and the methodology?

- Have the difficulties of the research been outlined and discussed?

- Is the research realistic about negative or neutral results?

- What contribution does the research make to the overall knowledge of the topic?

- What contribution might the research make to social work practice?

Reflection

- How do I feel about the research topic, the way it has been carried out and the findings?

- Why might I have responded to the research in this way?

- What are the implications of this for my thinking about the topic?

- What is the impact on my judgements about the research?

Overall

- What conclusions can I draw about the value of this research?

- In summary, what is the justification for this conclusion?

This is a rather long list and when considering pieces of research you may not answer every question. For instance, you may be reading a shortened account of the research in a journal article, rather than the whole research study. This may mean that not all the issues you wish to explore are discussed. However, it will assist your critical analysis skills if you aim to cover all these points.

ACTIVITY **9.2**

Critically analysing research

Select an article from British Journal of Social Work, Journal of Social Work *or* Critical Social Policy *on a topic which is relevant to either of your placements. Read it through once to get a general understanding. Then read it again using the questions above so as to develop a critical analysis.*

Nicola's placement

Nicola's second placement was in a general hospital and she was working mostly with older people. She was keen to look at relevant research and carried out a search of electronic journals using the term 'older people'. This yielded a number of articles from which she chose one initially because it was specifically about hospitals. Her practice assessor, Petra, reminded her she should take a critically analytic approach to her reading. Below we can see some of Nicola's thinking from using the list of questions. It is presented in note form but should enable you to see some results of critical analysis. You might find it helpful to read the article for yourself.

McLeod, E, Bywaters, P and Cooke, M (2003) Social work in accident and emergency departments : A better deal for older patients' health? British Journal of Social Work, *33 (6), 787–802.*

Research topic

The research refers to a good range of relevant literature including international work, many government publications and the researchers' own book. Some of this reading might also be useful to me, especially Littlechurch and Glasby (2000).

The article is about the study of older people – part of a larger project. A social worker was located in a hospital A and E department for six months with the aim of diverting inappropriate admissions. This research was over two months of this period. An interesting topic – the need for it is well argued by the authors.

A clear picture of the constraints of the broader context of health and social care is provided.

It has emancipatory focus aiming to highlight the experiences of older people in A an E.

Research question(s)

The article doesn't clearly say what the research question was – I assume it was What was the significance for older service users of the social work service they received while they were in A and E and immediately afterwards?

It was funded by the NHS – but no more detail is provided – given the funding source how independent was it?

Research ethics

Not mentioned apart from seeking consent for informal carers to be interviewed.

I assume it would have to meet the ethical requirements of the NHS trust.

No ethical dilemmas are discussed.

The conduct of the research

This was a small-scale qualitative pilot study. Hard to say if those interviewed were representative of older people seen in A and E.

It consisted of semi-structured telephone interviews of 28 older people (65–92 years) and informal carers, with consent, two to three weeks after treatment in A and E. But is telephone a good way of doing those? Might be cheaper but will it pick up non-verbal aspects of communication?

The interviews covered brief socio-biographical details, accounts of the circumstances leading to A and E attendance, experience in the hospital and of subsequent health and social care services, together with current health and social situations.

Methodology – not made specific but it seems to be a piece of action research/evaluation. It explored the impact of having a social worker in A and E though it does not mention changes to the role as a result of the ongoing research.

The methods were telephone interviews and social work records – though there was no discussion about the disadvantages or benefits of either.

Doesn't say who carried out the interviews or any difficulties (such as speech, language, hearing) or how the interviews were recorded.

Not clear how the data were analysed to identify the major themes. Quotes are used to illustrate the themes – how representative are they? Few statistics used. Maybe a few more would have strengthened this.

Social justice

An older people's forum in the city commented on the aims and approach. This was an interesting approach; I wonder if this could have been developed.

More women than men were interviewed; this was consistent with the age group.

Minority ethnic patients were under-represented compared to their proportion of the city's population – why? Suggests they are not referred to the social worker. This would merit more investigation. I am aware of the Joseph Rowntree Foundation Study (Butt and O'Neil, 2004) which highlights the problems older people from all BME groups face – waiting times on trolleys and for health care and lack of follow-up from hospital to home.

Aimed to get service users' feedback on a trend in health provision – trying to ensure the voices of older people are heard.

Was the larger research concerned with social justice for older people or to ensure the NHS works better and so saves money? If this is the case, can emancipatory research be carried out despite different agendas?

Findings

Four types of assistance from the social worker were welcomed: help with negotiating the demands of attending A and E; help with accessing social services department services;

home care; placements in intermediate care. Service users felt supported by the social worker.

However, a quarter of people had terminated the services provided by the social worker two to three weeks later because of their shortcomings – or because the elderly person had wanted to remain independent.

The figures showed a small drop in numbers discharged without follow-up service than the previous year and a rise in the proportion discharged from A and E without admission. The authors admit the statistical evidence is crude and the changes were not necessarily caused by the presence of the social worker.

Doesn't claim to be more than indicative but says it raises important issues which connect with the other literature mentioned.

Highlights broader issues; lack of referral to social worker especially BME groups; inadequate resources; professional/patient hierarchies; longer-term shortages.

Reflection

I found it terribly sad – the accounts of people's lives and situations – but it reflects some of what I have seen in the hospital and my friend's gran's experience so I was inclined to believe it.

I probably need to be a bit more systematic when looking at research so I don't only respond in an emotional way but also use my brain.

Overall

Some of the difficulties I have identified may arise from this being an article reporting a part of the research – so there wasn't space for some more detailed aspects of the study which would have been interesting. I would like to get hold of a fuller report.

In a small-scale way, despite some possible limitations in the way the research was carried out, this research highlights some important issues. It raises some concerns about the role of social workers. In this instance social workers were there to support older people through a hostile environment, to give information, to refer on to and to assist in planning care. I wondered whether social workers might not be needed if the health service operated in a more sensitive way. Is our role to ameliorate an unsympathetic and unresponsive system?

Reading this alerted me to some possible topics for my dissertation and maybe a piece of small-scale research.

This answer from Nicola is not intended to be a model answer but does show how a critical and questioning approach can be taken to research.

Critical application to practice

We now move to thinking in more detail about how research might guide social work practice. While this is recognised as necessary and important, it is not a routine activity in social work. Despite a number of initiatives and the greater accessibility of research information, the development of research-informed learning organisations in social work is still ongoing. Here a series of pointers towards becoming a research-informed student will be identified and an example provided.

Becoming research-informed

In your particular area of social work practice, develop the habits of:

- being enquiring about and alert to what research is currently available;
- regularly checking websites and keeping up to date;
- focusing on reliable and relevant sources;
- using research guidance and reviews.

In relation to specific topics or issues:

- search thoroughly – you may need to use various search terms to find what you need;
- access and read a range of material;
- be alert to the historical relevance and/or currency of the material.

Dealing with what you find:

- consider pieces of research in relation to others;
- take a critically analytic approach (as outlined above);
- try to identify whether the research study might relate to your specific and individual issue;
- consider whether the research material helps you to look at the situation differently;
- ask whether, and in what ways, the research might lead you to practise in a particular way.

ACTIVITY **9.3**

Becoming research-informed

Think of a practice issue in your second placement about which you wanted to know more or about which you had some uncertainties. Use the above approach to discover how research might provide some helpful indicators.

CASE STUDY

Dan's second placement

Here is an example of how Dan used this approach to develop his practice on a second placement in a children looked after team.

Awareness of existing research

From his previous employment and his college studies Dan had a general awareness that the educational outcomes for children looked-after by local authorities were below those of children in the general population. He was working with two young people aged 11 who were really struggling at school and he knew that other social workers in the team had the same experience. Dan had also been thinking about a lecture in college concerning the value of groupwork. He had been wondering whether it would be a good idea to set up a group with an educational focus for looked-after young people – maybe a homework group. His practice assessor, Ahmed, suggested that Dan should explore what research findings there were which could guide his thinking and inform a decision about this possibility.

Dan found his college reading list, went to the library and began searching for books, articles, policy documents and other relevant material. Here are some of his findings.

Children looked-after and education

- *There has been concern about the education of children looked after since the 1990s (Fawcett et al., 2004).*

- *The Green Paper* Care Matters *(DfES, 2006c) includes statistics which show that children in care perform less well at school than their peers at all stages. It also highlights the difficulties children face. Dan particularly noted that most schools only have a small number of children in care attending them and he wondered if they felt quite isolated. Another finding was that not all care placements replicate an engaged parent ensuring a good education for their child.*

- *The most recent statistics on children looked-after (year ending March 2007) show that the proportion of children looked after leaving care with at least one GCSE or GNVQ rose by only 1 per cent from 2006 to 2007 (from 43 to 44 per cent). The same was true for those leaving care with at least five GCSEs at grades A–C – the figure rose from 6 to 7 per cent (www.dcsf.gov.uk).*

- *The White Paper* Care Matters *(DfES, 2007) in relation to education, focuses on school admission, avoiding disruption to education, designated teachers, personalised learning and support for improved attendance.*

- *Research by the Social Exclusion Unit (SEU, 2003) identified five factors which would support children looked-after in their education: greater stability, less time out of school, help with schoolwork, more help from home to support schoolwork, improved health and well-being.*

- *Research carried out by* Voice for the Child in Care (VCC) *reported young people saying that encouragement from foster carers and residential workers was a key element in educational progress. Finding other areas for potential success inside and outside school were thought to be important (VCC, 2004a).*

- *Research carried out by VCC (2004b) in which looked after children from BME communities said they wanted to do well in education but felt stigmatised by the school system. They felt the school did not appreciate the massive difficulties in their lives.*

- *A research study on the post-care experiences of young people from different minority ethnic groups suggested that young people would have appreciated encouragement from their social worker in relation to all aspects of school, not just when there were problems; that financial input was not always forthcoming when needed (Barn et al., 2005).*

- *Accounts from young people in care which suggest the importance of social workers who made sure that additional educational support was in place and foster carers who valued education (Cree and Davis, 2007).*

- *Research which investigated the views of young people looked after who had done well academically and gone on to higher education. The findings were that:*

  - *the young people wanted to be like others, with opportunities to take part in hobbies and activities;*

  - *positive encouragement and active interest from significant adults was very important;*

  - *stability of placement was generally helpful, especially supportive foster care;*

  - *residential workers and foster carers should be well educated and qualified;*

  - *social workers should be in regular contact and show genuine concern for welfare;*

  - *attending school regularly was important;*

  - *negative stereotypes of looked-after children had to be overcome;*

  - *more support from teachers was needed;*

  - *placements lacked relevant practical resources;*

  - *all children looked after should have good support, not only those seen as very able;*

  - *there should be more support for higher education;*

  - *a special relationship with someone who made the young person feel valued, like a mentor, could be very helpful.*

  (Martin and Jackson, 2002; Jackson et al., 2005)

- *An account of an activity group for young people in care which aims to promote positive involvement in leisure activities, thereby increasing confidence and self-esteem – qualities which can impact on school attainment (Hopkins, 2004).*

- *An SCIE research summary on resilience in fostered young people published in Community Care, 24 May 2007. It noted that, after family, school was the most important thing to young people. Self-esteem which can be enhanced by feeling successful, not just academically, was an important resilience factor.*

Given the age of the young people, Dan might have looked at general research into young people and difficulties following transfer to secondary school. Dan has assumed that the problems the young people are facing are connected with their looked-after status – and this may be the case. Because there has been a huge emphasis on the education of children looked after, it seemed right to begin there. Arguably this investigation could have had a different starting point.

Dan found lots of material on the topic which wasn't directly pertinent to the focus of his concern. He learnt the importance of using abstracts and summaries and of skim-reading as means of assessing the relevance of the material. From the wealth of information he tried to sift out what really focused on what social workers can do to support children looked-after in education. Here we do not have the space to carry out the full critical analysis as we did with Nicola's research. Ahmed encouraged Dan to keep a record of the research findings and his critical analysis for discussion in supervision.

Groupwork

Dan also explored the social work literature on groupwork. However, research findings on groupwork with young people were limited. For example, in the groupwork project outlined in Doel (2006), only one group was held with children under 12. A useful article by Trevithick (2005b) identified that groupwork in social work is based on the interweaving of theoretical knowledge, factual knowledge and practice knowledge. The article also pointed out the gaps in knowledge in relation to the effectiveness of groupwork compared with work with individuals. From this reading Dan learnt that theories of groupwork suggest that groups can provide:

- a safe space to share common issues or problems;
- the opportunity for empowerment, and growth in self-esteem;
- the opportunity for change;
- a resource for learning.

Dan also used the literature to explore different models of groupwork; guidance on setting up groups and to read about practice examples (Mullender and Ward, 1991; Brown, 2002; Adams, 2003; Coulshed and Orme, 2006; Doel, 2006; Preston-Shoot, 2007).

From all this Dan reached the following conclusions:

- The education of children looked-after has been a longstanding problem and progress to improve matters is slow.
- Children and young people benefit from personal interest being shown in them and their achievements – someone who is ambitious for them.

- Research into groups might not give a clear steer on how to proceed with a group. However, social work textbooks provide groupwork theory, knowledge and useful guidance, integrating social work values, on how to run a group.

Dan's research-informed practice

Dan discussed all this in supervision with Ahmed. They wrestled with the problem of how to apply this generalised information to the specific situation Dan was concerned about. Dan felt that this exploration had given him a different perspective, particularly the research that suggested children looked-after benefited from someone being really interested in them and their achievements. So, rather than a very task-focused homework group he proposed a different approach. Drawing from, and building on, the research, Dan and Ahmed decided to set up an eight-week after-school activity group on Thursdays for six children looked-after aged 11–12 years. The aim would be to ensure that each young person had a significant success experience during that time. As far as possible the young people would make the decisions about ground rules and activities. Dan would also evaluate the group from different perspectives (those of the young people, workers and carers) and write an account for his portfolio. Hence Dan's decision about how to proceed was informed by research, particularly about resilience factors. Other relevant issues were groupwork theory, Dan's prior experience of young people and the social work value of empowerment.

C H A P T E R   S U M M A R Y

Here we have built on Chapter 8 to use higher-level academic skills in relation to research. This began with a discussion about the ethics of research and their significance in both carrying out and evaluating research. The tools for critical analysis of research were provided together with an extended example. We next considered how research might inform social work practice and a set of guidelines together with an example were presented. While the focus of the chapter has been on research, it is important to remember that, as Dan discovered, in some aspects of social work the research base is relatively weak. Further, research is not the only factor to take into account; it will need to be weighed up and incorporated with other factors when exploring a topic or planning social work practice interventions. In Chapters 11 and 12 we will include research findings along with theory, knowledge and values to appreciate the complexity of social work thinking and practice.

FURTHER READING

For a fuller account of social research ethics, see the following.

Gomm, R (2004) *Social research methodology: A critical introduction*. Basingstoke: Palgrave.

McLaughlin, H (2007) *Understanding social work research*. London: Sage (Chapter 4).

Chapter 10

Becoming an independent and autonomous learner

ACHIEVING A SOCIAL WORK DEGREE

This chapter will help you to meet the following National Occupational Standards.
Key Role 6: Demonstrate professional competence in social work practice.
- Work within agreed standards of social work practice and ensure own professional development.

It will introduce you to the following academic standards set out in the social work subject benchmark statement.
5.3 All social work honours graduates should show the ability to reflect on and learn from the exercise of their skills. They should understand the significance of concepts of continuing professional development and lifelong learning and accept responsibility for their own continuing development.
5.8 Honours graduates in social work should be able to:
- advance their own learning and understanding with a degree of independence.
- take responsibility for their own further and continuing acquisition of knowledge and skills.
5.5.3 Honours graduates in social work should be able to analyse and synthesise knowledge gained for problem solving purposes, i.e. to:
- assess human situations, taking into account a variety of factors (including the view of participants, theoretical concepts, research evidence, legislation and organisational policies and procedures)
- assess the merits of contrasting theories, explanations, research, policies and procedures.
5.8 Honours graduates should be able to:
- use research critically and effectively to sustain and develop their practice.

It will help you meet the Quality Assurance Agency for Higher Education (2001) requirement that students studying at Level 3 (H level) are able to demonstrate:
v. the ability to manage their own learning and to make use of scholarly reviews and primary sources, e.g. refereed research articles and/or original materials appropriate to the discipline;
and
a. apply the methods and techniques that they have learned to review, consolidate, extend and apply their knowledge and understanding and to initiate and carry out projects;
and will have
- the learning ability needed to undertake appropriate further training of a professional or equivalent nature.

Introduction

When you are studying at Level H of a degree, it is expected that the process, as well as the content, of your learning will be different and more complex than at the earlier levels. So it is important to give some attention to how you are studying. As you progress through the degree you should become aware of how you learn so that you are able to manage your own learning more fully – becoming an autonomous and independent learner. This means that you are able to self-direct your learning, needing less guidance, teaching and support. Another aspect of being an independent learner is appreciating that achieving the degree is one stage in your continuing professional development which will be part of being a social worker. Taking an active role in this means being able to identify your future learning needs. This awareness of and reflection on how you learn, appreciation of your learning needs and ability to respond appropriately is known as metacognition. In this chapter different aspects of metacognition will be explored.

After reading this chapter you should be able to:

• appreciate how to become a more independent learner;

• reflect on and identify how you learn;

• understand the importance of, and your role in, continuing professional development.

Becoming an independent learner

On your course the assignments and learning activities will be designed to support you in moving towards independence in learning so that by the third year you should be self-directing and autonomous. In particular, when you are working on your final project or dissertation, there is an expectation that you work with a high level of independence. Here we will identify the attributes of an independent and autonomous learner and consider the value of reflection in moving towards an understanding of both how you learn and areas for developmental growth.

ACTIVITY 10.1

The characteristics of an independent and autonomous learner

List what you think are the characteristics of an independent and autonomous learner. Then compare your list with the points in the research summary.

The characteristics of an independent and autonomous learner

Taking responsibility for your own learning: *taking charge of your own learning and acting independently; being less reliant on tutors and classes for your learning; not using as much guidance and support. It means recognising that you learn in a different way from other people, so you will need to choose your own direction; formulate your own problems; decide on your course of action.*

Having an engaged disposition towards learning and understanding learning as an active process: *not passively receiving and reproducing material but engaging with ideas, identifying relationships and interconnections; building on what you know, interpreting, restructuring and transforming your understanding as you learn more; appreciating that you will need to put mental effort into making personal sense of new information and experiences. It also involves seeing learning as continuous, ongoing, and lifelong.*

Actively participating in supervision and tutorials: *thinking ahead to supervision and tutorials, identifying the guidance and direction you need; being prepared with questions, issues, ideas and suggestions; actively contributing to discussion and debate.*

Using feedback, both positive and negative: *carefully reading and assimilating feedback; ensuring you understand what it means; allowing yourself to be challenged by it; working out what you need to do as a result and implementing this.*

Setting your own learning goals: *being clear about your long-term objectives; identifying short-term goals which will help you work towards the objectives; monitoring your progress towards meeting the goals; making adjustments if necessary.*

Developing key study skills and strategies which work for you: *this might be time management; strategies for reading or writing.*

Being self monitoring: *knowing what are effective ways of studying for you, what are not, and planning your study accordingly. Sternberg and Zhang (2001) note that this is one constructive component of the strategic approach to learning (see Chapter 1).*

Discovering your own learning resources: *independently exploring sources of knowledge and research; being able to make informed judgements about the value of resources.*

Seeking out, being alert to and recognising learning opportunities: *in college, on your placement and in other aspects of your life.*

Being self-aware and self-evaluating: *learning to judge and evaluate your own thinking and writing will develop creativity and self-reliance. You should also be able to identify your own progress in learning.*

Developing confidence in your own judgements: *in order to develop as an independent learner, students need to have realistic confidence and self-esteem. Lack of self-belief and anxiety can get in the way of motivation and effective learning.*

(Gibbs,1981; Eraut, 1994; Macaulay, 2000; Chan, 2001; Biggs, 2003; Clare, 2007)

This is an ambitious list of the characteristics of the ideal learner. However, all these attributes will tend to feed into and reinforce each other, thereby developing your capacity to learn. If you work on one it should support the development of others. Many of these attributes are transferable to social work practice and the characteristics expected of a professional practitioner.

ACTIVITY **10.2**

Self-evaluation

Looking at the list above, evaluate yourself as an independent and autonomous learner. Think about this in relation to both college and your placement. Identify areas for development.

CASE STUDY

Dan's self-evaluation

At the first tutorial for his dissertation, Dan was asked by his tutor to think about how far he had progressed as an independent learner. This is his self-evaluation using the headings set out above.

Taking responsibility for your own learning. *From where I started on the course, when I was a bit dismissive about college learning, I have come to love classes and tutorials. I think this change has forced me into thinking about how I learn. I now approach college learning in a much more open way and spend a lot of time thinking about it and turning it over in my mind.*

Having an active disposition towards learning and understanding learning as an active process. *When I am mulling things over in my mind (usually on car journeys home from college) I am relating college teaching to my experiences at work and on placement. And it works the other way round too. My whole attitude towards learning has changed. I really work at trying to make sense of things. My partner teases me about this – I question everything now.*

Actively participating in supervision and tutorials. *I am now very active in tutorials but could do more to prepare for them – I can see how this would make the use of this time more productive. I plan to improve on this for my dissertation.*

Using feedback both positive and negative. *I started off being a bit of a 'know-all' and not always taking feedback seriously (in my mind I would always be answering back 'yes but...'). Now I appreciate that if I read feedback, go back and read through the assignment in the light of the comments and try to implement the advice, then my work has really improved.*

Setting your own learning goals. *For some reason this is a hard one for me. As I have become more enthusiastic about learning I have tended to get carried away on issues that interest me, rather then working more methodically. For my dissertation I will draw up a time plan for the whole piece of work with short-term and long-term goals.*

CASE STUDY *continued*

Developing key study skills and strategies which work for you. *I'm still working on this. When I started the course I was so focused on the goal of getting a qualification that I used study skills which got the work in on time but didn't always develop my learning. Then I went the other way – my aim for the dissertation is to find a better balance.*

Being self-monitoring. *I'm getting much better at understanding myself, what I'm doing and why, pushing myself to change if necessary and trying out different ways of bringing about change. The session I had with my training officer was really helpful in supporting me to understand why I was struggling with the course and what changes I needed to make.*

Discovering your own learning resources. *I now love spending time searching for resources though I am not always very well focused on this. I can get carried away and don't always use my time well. It has taken me a while to be able to work out the relative value of different sources of research and information. I need to work on this, especially for my dissertation.*

Seeking out, being alert to and recognising learning opportunities. *This has been a big shift for me – it feels as if I can hardly stop learning.*

Being self-aware and self-evaluating. *I am making progress but there is room for development here. I think I could be more rigorous. My tendency is to leave it to tutors and my practice assessor to highlight the weaknesses in my work.*

Developing confidence in your own judgements. *At times on the course my confidence in myself has taken a severe knock. I thought I was really a gift to the college. Now I see I was a bit arrogant about my experience and superficial in my learning. Discovering that my approach wouldn't get me through the course, and was not OK, was a real shock. I hope I have worked hard, with people's help, to change and to develop a clearer sense of myself. I think the more balanced appreciation of my strengths and weaknesses, which has been the outcome, provides me with a sounder base from which to make judgements. It was important for me to go through this process as a student, professionally and personally. And a bonus is that I have been told I am now easier to live with!*

Metacognition

One way of making progress as an independent learner is to develop your skills in metacognition. This means:

- conscious awareness of your own learning capacity and your experience of learning;

- your ability to articulate this – being able to explain how you have learnt and transformed your understanding;

- using this to monitor and adjust your approach to learning and problem-solving – to choose, revise or abandon learning strategies.

(Eraut, 1994; Stephenson, 2001; Jackson, 2004; Moon, 2005)

In Chapter 2 we considered the value of reflection in developing your social work practice. Here we are using reflection for a slightly different purpose: to understand and develop your metacognition. Moon (2004, 2005) suggests that you need to be able to stand back from yourself, not think about what you have learnt but rather the cognitive processes. This might mean reflecting on how you tackled a task, what are the ingredients when things are going well, what is going on when they are not – and why. Recognising the significance of the impact of our emotions was noted as an important aspect of reflection on practice. Similarly, in reflection on learning, the role of feelings must be considered for they connect to your motivation, your mood and your level of self-worth. All of these will impact on how you learn.

ACTIVITY 10.3

One way of reflecting on learning

Identify one learning experience, for example: a piece of written work in which you were asked to make a judgement; researching literature to understand an issue in more depth; engaging in a debate in college or using theory on placement to inform how to work with a service user.

Describe the learning experience using the following questions.

What happened? What were the main components of the experience?

This is the content of the experience. To really engage in reflection you need to move on to thinking about the process of the experience.

Reflect on how you learnt using these questions.

What was I trying to achieve?

Why did I go about it in the way I did?

How was I feeling? What impact did this have?

How did my previous experiences of learning affect how I felt and what I did?

How successful was this learning?

What factors helped to make this successful?

What was the impact of the way I went about this?

What other choices did I have?

What might have been the consequences of the other choices?

Learning from the experience; you could ask yourself these questions.

How do I feel now about the experience?

Could I have dealt with it differently?

What have I learnt from this which I might be able to use in new situations?

What might get in the way of my doing things differently?

Comment

We discussed ways of developing reflection for practice in Chapter 7. Similarly, when reflecting on your learning, a journal, a critical friend, supervision and tutorials can all be helpful. For instance, sometimes your tutor will be able to support you in thinking about the way you have gone about a learning task.

Moon (2004) argues that second-order reflection can further enhance reflection. This means taking a piece of reflective writing already completed and considering it in order to write a deeper reflective overview. By doing this you should be able to identify the impact of your attitudes towards a particular topic or of particular emotional states and how these might have shifted with different understanding. In this way you can act as your own critical friend.

CASE STUDY

Nicola's internet search: reflection and second-order reflection

Shortly before she went on her second placement, Nicola was carrying out an internet search to find material on the abuse of vulnerable adults for a college presentation.

Afterwards Nicola wrote reflectively.

> *I wanted to collect some literature which would help me to put together a ten-minute class presentation on the abuse of vulnerable adults I was due to give the following week. So I tried different search terms and different websites. I either got loads of hits or nothing. I had avoided working on this and focused on a different piece of work, because of my anxiety about doing a presentation – but also maybe because I didn't want to think about this topic. So I ended up doing the search at home with my teenage children nagging me because they wanted to use the computer and giving me unhelpful advice about Wikipedia. This stressed me out more. My partner Kieran had offered to cook the dinner but I thought I could smell burning from the kitchen. Distracted, I kept making silly mistakes and losing my way. Previously in college I had managed searches with reasonable success – although I knew I needed more practice. In this situation I found it hard to build on the skills I had learnt and make progress.*

> *But I think the biggest obstacle to my making progress was the topic. When we dealt with the general topic of vulnerability and abuse in college, we covered a range of service user groups. I found it very upsetting. Some of the categories of abuse made me feel sick. I didn't talk to anyone about this but knew I was full of dread about having to explore it more. This is probably why I had left it rather late and was almost sabotaging the research by the timing and circumstances. After finding a few relevant articles from Community Care I gave up, let the children use the computer and went to the kitchen, where I criticised Kieran's cooking and had a glass of wine. So that night I didn't sleep well because I hadn't successfully done the search and knew I shouldn't have taken it out on Kieran.*

CASE STUDY *continued*

Learning from the experience

I now feel a bit silly for doing what I did. After the college class I knew I had some sorting out to do in my own head. What we learnt made me think that my nan might have been abused by my grandad. How could I possibly have started researching the abuse of vulnerable adults without processing this? Even in the best of circumstances I would have struggled and I set up for myself the worst of circumstances and nearly risked a big family upset. I also knew that I was soon to start a placement in a hospital social work team, mostly working with older people so my anxiety about that was sky high. Obviously I could, and should, have found a better time and place to carry out the search. I now feel disappointed and cross with myself – I thought I had learnt more than this on the course.

Later Nicola used her critical friend Mandy for some second-order reflection

A week later Nicola showed Mandy what she had written. Mandy was really helpful in pointing out that, when Nicola wrote the account, her self-esteem was low because of her disappointment with herself. She suggested that Nicola was at risk of getting stuck in despair and reminded her of all the positive things she had achieved on the course. She helped Nicola reframe the experience so it could be used constructively to develop Nicola's learning.

Nicola noted that in future she would try to be more self-aware, more conscious of her emotions and not block them. She thought that exploring her feelings could be a useful tool for learning and she needed to find an appropriate place to do this. She wondered if by starting the search in the way she did, she had wanted unconsciously to share her upset, which she could not communicate openly, with the whole family. This led on to more thinking and learning about people in distress and the many indirect ways they let other people know this. When Nicola was on her placement she found this learning really helpful.

Future learning

By the end of the social work degree, as an independent and autonomous learner, you should be able to appreciate and articulate your learning journey. This means first thinking about how far you have travelled since you began your course; what you have learnt; how you have learned to learn; your personal and professional growth; the skills and qualities you have developed. Thinking about this reflectively can be rewarding and affirming. While you are studying, the demands of the course and the need to complete the next assignment can often get in the way of taking stock, appreciating how and why you have developed. At the final stage of the course you should complete the section of your personal development plan (PDP), which we first discussed in Chapter 1, to make sense of your experience and record your achievements. It can be very useful to work with a critical friend or a tutor to help you clarify your thinking and identify your growth and development. You might find it helpful to look back to your answers to Activity 1.1 of Chapter 1 as a reminder of yourself when you started the course.

Second, you need to give some attention to the learning journey ahead of you together with your needs and goals for continuing learning and development. When you reach the end of the course it may seem as if you have reached the end of your journey. However, for practising professionals learning is a lifelong process – you will need to go on acquiring and updating knowledge and skills, exploring values and adapting to change. Further, the social work degree is generic. While your training and education have provided you with a qualification to work in any field of social work and you will have specific expertise from your placement settings, this will not be sufficient for your career. To survive and thrive, in the particular field of social work where you gain employment, you will need specialist knowledge and understanding. Being able to appreciate your future learning needs is a fundamental aspect of being an autonomous learner. These too should be recorded on your personal development plan.

Thoughtfully and thoroughly completing your PDP will provide you with a record of your achievement and your future learning needs in a document you can share with prospective employers, demonstrating your understanding of the importance of continuing profes-sional development.

ACTIVITY 10.4

My development as a learner

As you approach the end of the course try to summarise:

- *the personal development you have achieved through the course;*

- *how you have developed professionally through the course (knowledge, skills, values);*

- *your learning needs during the next three years.*

CASE STUDY

Saranita's development

The personal development I have achieved through the course

I have grown up a lot. Being with mostly mature students, some old enough to be my mother, has taught me lots about learning from experience. I think these are the important issues.

- *Being able now to share experiences and learn from others – this happened a lot, especially in the BME support group.*

- *Being more self-managing – not needing to seek guidance all the time but knowing when it is important to do so.*

- *I have developed in confidence in speaking in the group and challenging when neces-sary – this includes presenting different perspectives on race and culture to those being presented by the tutor.*

My professional development

I was very inexperienced professionally when I started the course and didn't realise this. Because of my age and relative lack of some life experiences, I still have a long way to go. The most significant learning has been:

- *really being able to grasp theory and use it to guide my practice;*

- *appreciating research, especially by carrying out the small study in my second placement;*

- *having a much deeper understanding of discrimination and its impact on people's lives – especially poverty;*

- *letting go of my need to do everything for people and shifting towards a more empowering way of doing social work;*

- *developing my interpersonal skills – understanding how other people may perceive me and knowing how to present myself in different situations – but still be me.*

My learning needs during the next three years

I have been offered a post in the Children's Centre where I was on my second placement so my learning needs will mostly be related to my employment. I have identified them as:

- *enhancing my assessment and observation skills, particularly in everyday and less formal situations;*

- *developing my groupwork skills – there will be lots of opportunities for this;*

- *building a deeper understanding of safeguarding children and factors which promote resilience;*

- *continuing to improve my skills in listening well to people – this links to developing a more empowering style of social work.*

Continuing professional development

Once you have completed the course, you will need to register as a qualified social worker with the General Social Care Council (GSCC). It is a requirement of registration that you complete, over a three-year period, 90 hours or 15 days of study, training, courses, seminars, reading, teaching or other activities to enhance and advance your professional development. This is known as Post Registration Training and Learning (PRTL). You must keep a record of this, setting out both the details of the learning activity and some reflection on how it has contributed to your training and learning. Your employer has a responsibility to support your undertaking your PRTL to enable you to develop in your work role. When you start as a qualified social worker, this might be induction training to assist in taking on your new post. Later in your career it might involve supporting you to undertake post-qualifying training (www.gscc.org.uk).

Of course, continuing professional development has benefits additional to meeting the requirements of the GSCC. It can provide a way of keeping a balanced perspective in the uncertain, demanding, shifting and uncertain world of social work practice. It enables you to maintain contact with current research, theories and ideas. While keeping you up to date it should also be stimulating and provide material for reflection on your practice (Eraut, 1994; Lishman, 1998).

CHAPTER SUMMARY

This chapter has focused on learning at Level H of an undergraduate degree in social work. We have explored what it means to be an autonomous, independent learner and seen how it is relevant at this stage of your study. In particular we focused on metacognition, a facet of learning which can be promoted through reflection. The attributes of an independent, autonomous learner identified here will be required for the final stages of your study – on most courses this will involve writing a dissertation or completing another kind of independent project. We will explore this in more depth in Chapter 12. Implicit in this understanding of learning is that you will continue your professional development into and throughout your employment. By the end of your social work degree you should be ready to be a lifelong learner.

FURTHER READING

Cottrell, S (2003) *The study skills handbook*. 2nd edition. Basingstoke: Palgrave.
This helpful book includes practical suggestions for managing your own study.
To find out more about GSCC registration, the Post Registration Training and Learning requirements and post-qualifying programmes, access the website for the GSCC, www.gscc.org.uk.

Cooper, B (2008) Continuing professional development a critical approach. In **Fraser, S and Mathews, S** *The critical practitioner in social work and health care*. London: Sage, pp222–37.
A useful exploration of the current model of continuing professional development.

Chapter 11

Dealing with complexity: Using knowledge in practice

This chapter will help you to meet the following National Occupational Standard.
Key Role 6: Demonstrate professional competence in social work practice.
- Research, analyse, evaluate and use current knowledge of best social work practice.
- Work within agreed standards of social work practice and ensure own professional development.
- Manage complex ethical dilemmas and conflicts.

It will introduce you to the following academic standards set out in the social work subject benchmark statement:
5.1 During their degree studies in social work, honours graduates should acquire, critically evaluate, apply and integrate knowledge and understanding in the following five core areas of study.
5.1.1 Social work services, service users and carers.
5.1.2 The service delivery context.
5.1.3 Values and ethics which includes
- The complex relationships between justice, care and control in social welfare and the practical and ethical implications of these, including roles as statutory agents and in upholding the law in respect of discrimination.
5.1.4 Social work theory.
5.1.5 The nature of social work practice.
5.8 Honours graduates should be able to
- manage uncertainty, change and stress in work situations.
- understand and manage changing situations and respond in a flexible manner.
- reflect on and modify their behaviour in the light of experience.

It will help you meet the Quality Assurance Agency for Higher Education (2001) requirement that students studying at Level 3 (H level) are able to demonstrate:
iii. conceptual understanding that enables the student
- to devise and sustain arguments and /or to solve problems using ideas and techniques, some of which are at the forefront of a discipline and
- to describe and comment upon particular aspects of current research, or equivalent advanced scholarship, in the discipline
iv. an appreciation of the uncertainty, ambiguity and limits of knowledge;
and
a. critically evaluate arguments, assumptions, abstract concepts and data (that may be incomplete) to make judgements, and to frame appropriate questions to achieve a solution – or identify a range of solutions – to a problem;
b. communicate information, ideas, problems and solutions to both specialist and non-specialist audiences.

Introduction

One factor in the decision that social work should become a graduate profession was the recognition that sophisticated academic skills were needed for competent practice. This was acknowledgement of the complexity of current social work practise in which critical, analytic and reflective ability is required to practise with confidence. In this chapter we will discuss some aspects of this complexity before considering strategies for using higher-level academic skills constructively to support positive ways of working in this environment.

After reading this chapter you should be able to:

- appreciate the reasons for the complexity of social work practice;

- identify some skills and strategies for working within complexity.

The complex nature of social work

We will begin by considering in more detail the nature of current social work practice, focusing on three aspects: the context of practice, ethical dilemmas and the contested nature of knowledge. At this stage of your course you should have a sound awareness of such issues, from both your studies and your placement. Our discussion here will build on these themes covered in earlier chapters – the aim is to help you to make better sense of your experiences.

The context of practice

Commentators writing about contemporary social work have described it as *messy, chaotic, contradictory* (Macaulay, 2000, p21); *ambiguous, complex, uncertain* (Parton, 2000, p452); *working with some of the most complex problems and perplexing areas of human experience* (Trevithick, 2005a, p1): *uncertain, demanding, complex and changing* (Lishman, 1998, p89). This view is shared by practitioners who are confronted with this context in their lived experience of day-to-day work:

> *I work with challenging, difficult and complex situations and on a daily basis have to plan, prioritise, organise and motivate myself. (Chima, 2003, p17)*

> *...there is currently a great deal of uncertainty and anxiety, as well as excitement, about what the future may hold. (Merton, 2003, p49)*

Schön (1983, p42), writing more generally about professional practice, graphically describes it as *the swampy lowland where situations are confusing 'messes'*. He also asserts that this is where that the greatest problems of human concern for practitioners occur.

In order to develop ways of working in the current, challenging context, it can be helpful to first develop an analysis of the reasons for this.

ACTIVITY **11.1**

Understanding the context of social work practice analytically

Identify some explanations for the state of current social work practice. Then compare with the analysis set out below.

I suggest there are six possible interlocking explanations.

1. *Rapid policy and legal changes*. The uncertain context of social work practice is defined by the swift pace of a changing policy and legal framework. Such change relates both to social work and the wider social welfare sphere such as benefits, education, housing, health and education (Lishman, 1998; Lymbery and Butler, 2004). Particular aspects of these changes which contribute to the complexity of the policy context are marketisation, privatisation, globalisation, modernisation, the social investment state, performativity and stakeholding (Trevillion, 2000; Jones, 2001; Garrett, 2003; Fawcett et al., 2004). The nature of these policy shifts also potentially changes the relationship of the individual to the state and thus also impacts on the identity of social work practice. It requires practitioners to be clear about their role in changing times (Butler and Drakeford, 2001).

2. *Considerable organisational change*. The agencies in which social work is practised have undergone, and continue to be in the process of, huge structural changes. This includes a stream of government initiatives, local government reorganisation and the setting up of health trusts, care trusts, integrated health and social care services and children's services departments (Horner, 2006). The impact of this on social workers can, unsettlingly, be experienced as *permanent reorganisation* (Cree and Davis, 2007, p156), or as Trevillion (2000, p511) puts it, *no one map of the world is reliable*.

3. *Challenges to the role and purpose of social work*. Debates about the role and purpose of social work have consistently underlain its practice. Current tensions in the role are between:

   - a focus on the alleviation of individual distress and misery and on challenging structural oppression;
   - promoting empowerment, and ensuring the protection of vulnerable children and adults;
   - concern for the welfare of individuals and carrying out functions of social control;
   - bureaucracy and procedures and creativity.

   Arguably these challenges to the role and purpose of social work have been exacerbated by the findings of public inquiries into scandals in social care provision and the deaths of children (Lishman, 1998; Lymbery and Butler, 2004; Payne, 2005; Horner, 2006).

4. *Social workers are increasingly working with people with severe and deep-seated difficulties*. As the threshold criteria for services are set higher, social workers are more and more working with service users and carers in complex circumstances with multiple

difficulties. This is further complicated by an increasing gap between welfare systems and individual need (Trevillion, 2000; Jones, 2001; Lymbery and Butler, 2004; Cree and Davis, 2007;).

5. *Contradictions between policy and practice*. Sometimes social workers experience a contradiction between declared policies and actual practice. This might mean, for instance, that the way people within the organisation are treated is inconsistent with equal opportunities policies (Charles and Butler, 2004). In Chapter 2 we learnt how Saranita had observed a dissonance between the values set out in the National Service Framework for Older People and the experience of patients in the hospital. It might also mean the gap between what welfare systems claim to provide and the reality, where social need is not met. The position of social workers, mediating between service users and organisations, can mean that they experience such gaps and contradictions acutely.

6. *The constraints imposed by resource limitations*. In practice social workers find that their ability to work with service users can be constrained by their own workloads and lack of time, but also by the budgetary limits and insufficiency of other resources. A student social worker in Ford et al.'s (2005, p402) study expressed it this way, echoing the experience of many practitioners:

> ...time limits of things and when we are supposed to do things, how much time we're supposed to spend with people and doing risk assessments and, in reality, you're out there and there isn't the time to do them...budgets don't allow for certain ways of practising...and a lot of it comes down to time constraints and budget restraints really.

These six factors combine to create a context for practice which will by now undoubtedly be familiar to you.

ACTIVITY *11.2*

Examples from your placement

For each of the six explanations given for the challenging nature of current social work practice, identify an example from your placement.

Ethical dilemmas in social work practice

We first explored values in Chapter 2, considered their fundamental importance to social work practice and noted the role of the shared set of values set out in the Code of Practice for Social Care Workers (GSCC, 2002). In practice, despite the clarity of the code, students and social workers can find that integrating values into their work is not so straightforward and they are often posed with ethical dilemmas. In such situations social workers are faced with two or more apparently contradictory values; they need to be able to find a way forward which takes both into account. This might involve balancing:

- an individual's right to self-determination with potential risk to themself or others;
- the needs and wishes of a service user with different needs and wishes of their carer;

- respecting confidentiality with sharing information with colleagues and other agencies;

- their own values with social work values;

- empowering service users with having the capacity to exercise power in their lives;

- obligations to service users with accountability to the agency.

ACTIVITY 11.3

Identifying an ethical dilemma

Identify an ethical dilemma you have come across in practice. Write down the competing values which you found you were trying to resolve.

CASE STUDY

Dan's ethical dilemma

On his second placement in the children looked after team, Dan had worked for three months with Cammie, a 16-year-old young woman who had been subject to a care order since she was 12. Her time in care had been not been smooth; she had lived with several foster families and been excluded from school. However, for the past few months she seemed more settled in a residential unit and was studying for GCSEs at the local further education college. The view of most professionals who knew Cammie was that this progress was fragile and that minor setbacks could be major threats to her apparent stability. At her review Cammie said she wanted to move to independent accommodation, which in this local authority could mean a small flat. While he empathised with Cammie's desire for more autonomy and space, in which to express herself and develop, Dan had concerns about this plan. His assessment of Cammie was that she needed more everyday living skills and that she was vulnerable to exploitation by others, especially men. At the review the independent chair asked Dan to explore the issues more with Cammie. Before he did this Dan tried to identify the competing values, which he summarised as:

Cammie's right to independence, self-determination and respect for her wishes versus potential risk to her and particularly to the progress she had made.

All social work knowledge is contested

The third, related, factor contributing to the complexity of social work is that no aspect of knowledge in social work is straightforward or universally accepted – it is always debated. Beresford and Croft (2001) note the different types of knowledge in social work – theory, research, practitioner knowledge and service user knowledge. At this stage of your course, you should be aware that theory and research are contested – this was explored earlier in the book. In Chapter 3 we noted the limitations of and debates concerning theory. The debates concerning the value of the knowledge that different types of research can produce were discussed in Chapters 8 and 9. Throughout the book we have discussed the significance of practitioner knowledge or practice wisdom. The importance of understanding drawn from experience was highlighted in Chapter 6 and in Chapter 7 we considered the development of practitioner knowledge through reflection. In the first chapter of the book we noted the importance of the voices from, and perspectives of, people who use services and carers and the alternative views they can provide.

Hence we can see that knowledge for practice is constructed from a range of sources and this may not provide certainty or clarity (Payne, 2006). For students who are seeking definitive, concrete answers this could be problematic because some of these accounts will be competing versions and interpretations (Taylor and White, 2006). Put simply, a service user's account of the intervention by a social worker will be different from the social worker's. However, as Barnett (1994) points out, the mark of a student in higher education is their ability to recognise that what counts as truth can be seen from a number of different perspectives. Recognising the source of the knowledge, critical awareness of how it has been constructed and what that means for its use, is required of degree level students.

In Chapter 12 we will look in more depth at understanding a topic in different ways drawing on different sources.

Working in and with complexity

In this section we will identify some ways of thinking and practising in the complexity outlined in the first section. All of these approaches build on academic skills already covered in the book – skills in evaluation, analysis, reflection and critical thinking. Without these abilities you will find it difficult to make progress and successfully study at Level H of the social work degree. If you find yourself struggling, you might therefore find it useful to revisit earlier chapters.

Aim to be 'secure in unknowingness'

The complexity and uncertainty of social work have been explored above. Because there is a tendency to want the comfort of certainty, working in this context can be anxiety-provoking. One response to this unease can be unhelpful, concrete thinking which may mean neglecting to consider an issue from different perspectives using a range of knowledge and competing theoretical explanations. It is therefore important for students and social workers to develop the capacity to live with not knowing; appreciating that there may not be a correct answer; and actively seeking out and embracing other knowledges and versions of the truth. In this way complexity of understanding will be developed. This can have real practice significance as it can help avoid inappropriate certainty about the judgement of situations. An example of this is provided by Taylor and White (2006), who discuss the report into the death of Victoria Climbié (Laming, 2003, 6, p608). In this report the importance of an approach of 'respectful uncertainty' in relation to accounts of injuries was advocated as necessary for good practice – rather than social workers taking accounts at face value as had occurred. The aim of staying in respectful uncertainty, is consistent with the values of social work because it incorporates having regard for people's accounts. But it also avoids social workers using information and theory to justify decisions already made and rushing to judgement.

However, this approach also means learning to manage the anxiety generated by not having a clear solution, developing the ability to live with doubt and uncertainty while taking the time to seek other accounts.

RESEARCH SUMMARY

In a study by Clare (2007, p440), the learning of a group of Australian social work students was explored. She found that an important aspect of their development was a realisation that for professional practice they needed to learn 'secure unknowingness'. Students described being able to live in the uncertainty of not knowing all the answers nor having a fixed way ahead. Deep learning together with cognitive and emotional work on the course had helped them develop this confidence to be open to different perspectives and living with doubt.

For some students, learning to practise in this way may be anxiety-provoking. Managing such powerful emotions will be assisted by self-reflection and constructive use of supervision.

ACTIVITY 11.4

Working in uncertainty

Think about your ability to work in secure unknowingness. Reflect on how you respond to lack of certainty and the impact on your practice.

CASE STUDY

Petra's work with Mr Simpson

During Nicola's placement in the hospital social work team she came across Mr Simpson, an 80-year-old man in the early stages of Alzheimer's disease. Nicola's practice assessor, Petra, was the allocated social worker and she suggested Nicola observe some of her work to extend her experience. Normally Mr Simpson lived with his 50-year-old daughter but he had been in a respite residential home for two weeks when he was admitted to hospital after a fall. Ward staff found bed sores and what seemed to be old bruising and healed burns. Nicola was distressed by this and secretly felt that decisive action should be taken – she tended to assume that it was the residential home staff who were responsible. However, she observed that Petra took a more measured approach and was able to manage the uncertainty of not knowing. It transpired that there were differing accounts of the situation from:

Mr Simpson's daughter;

Mr Simpson's granddaughter;

the manager of the residential home;

the staff in the unit at the residential home;

other residents;

>
> *nurses on the ward;*
>
> *the psycho-geriatrician.*
>
> *In addition to all this Petra added her knowledge of:*
>
> *vulnerable older people;*
>
> *the law;*
>
> *the vulnerable adults policy;*
>
> *Alzheimer's disease;*
>
> *carers' experiences of looking after someone with Alzheimer's;*
>
> *and her commitment to the values of:*
>
> *respecting Mr Simpson' s rights;*
>
> *protecting Mr Simpson from abuse and harm.*
>
> *During this process Nicola felt worried and uncomfortable; she found she was dreaming about Mr Simpson and waking in the night thinking about him. She discussed this with Mandy, her critical friend, and explained that she just wanted it sorted out. Through their discussions Nicola began to understand better her feelings. She identified other situations in which she had been anxious and began to understand her deep-seated need for certainty. She talked about this with her college tutor and with Petra. Although it was not easy, once she had named what she was experiencing, she began to think of ways of dealing with it. She found that her ability to manage a variety of perspectives was assisted by recording them and using a diagram to understand how they connected.*

Use your thinking skills to resolve ethical dilemmas

Working within the complexity of social work you will find you need to find resolutions to ethical dilemmas. This can be a difficult balancing act; using the following steps may help you to use your analytic and creative thinking skills.

Spell out the competing values and think about the principles behind them

It can be helpful to clearly set out the competing positions and the principles that lie behind them – so understanding why this is a social work value.

Articulate the implications of different courses of action

Use your analytic thinking to identify the implications of the different courses of action implicit in each value position.

Work with people who use services and carers

It is a demonstration of respect to people who use services and carers if your developing thinking is shared with them in clear and understandable ways. When consulted, people who use services and carers said they wanted social workers to:

- *be open and honest about what they can and cannot do;*
- *involve users and carers in decision-making;*
- *be accountable to users and carers for their practice.*

(TOPSS, 2002b).

Build on your developing knowledge and experience to employ professional judgements

Banks (2006) suggests that, in a situation of competing values, experience can assist in making decisions about which value should take priority over another. As your social work career progresses you will be more able to judge whether learning from another situation can be helpfully deployed in new circumstances. Eraut (1994) argues that it is this interpretation of and application of learning and experience which constitutes professional judgement. Such expertise involves innovation and artistry as well as critical and analytic thinking and social workers also need to use creativity in resolving dilemmas and finding ways forward.

Knowing why you have chosen a particular course of action

You should be able to articulate your chosen course of action and justify it, clearly spelling out your reasons.

CASE STUDY

Dan's ethical dilemma about Cammie

Dan thought very carefully and reflectively about the piece of work the independent chair had asked him to do and discussed it in supervision. Together he and Ahmed, his practice assessor, reiterated the competing values – Cammie's right to independence, self-determination and respect for her wishes versus potential risk to her and particularly to the progress she had made. They considered whether the principles of self-determination should be modified in relation to teenagers – and if so, how. They discussed their duty to protect Cammie from danger but appreciated that Cammie also needed to learn how to protect herself from harm.

Dan reflected on himself and the dilemma. He was aware that one factor in his thinking was his wish for continuing good progress for Cammie, not only for her, but also because it might be evidence of his skills. He was pleased with the work they had done together. At the review he had been rather surprised when Cammie explained her wishes, as she had not discussed them with him. So he wondered if he was feeling disgruntled because he felt excluded from Cammie's decision.

Eventually Dan came up with an idea which he hoped would demonstrate respect to Cammie and be a helpful way of exploring the possibility of independent living. Dan, Cammie and her key worker from the residential home, Joy, sat together and individually wrote on sticky notes:

the gains for Cammie if she moved into a flat;

> **CASE STUDY** *continued*
>
> *what Cammie might lose;*
>
> *the opportunities that might open up;*
>
> *the risks to Cammie's well being.*
>
> *They arranged all these on flipchart sheets to build up a picture of the different views on the proposal and then discussed the issues raised at length. From the activity Cammie had a clear sense of the genuine concern of professionals for her well-being. Dan and Joy were a little surprised by Cammie's sound grasp of the potential risks. Out of the activity came a compromise that Cammie would postpone the request for six months, but take active steps to develop and demonstrate skills for managing a flat – with some support from Joy.*

Not all dilemmas will find such resolution. Often social work means living with the uncertainty and ambiguity outlined above.

> ACTIVITY **11.5**
>
> ### *Resolving your ethical dilemma*
>
> *In relation to the ethical dilemma you identified earlier, use the steps outlined above to identify how you found a resolution.*

Reflection in action

The third way in which practising within complexity can be developed is through the use of reflection in action. In Chapter 7 we explored in some depth the notion of reflection on action – thinking through an event after it has occurred. Reflection in action involves thinking things through reflectively while also taking part in them. An example might be reflection during a meeting with a service user, in a case review or while having a telephone conversation. It is one attribute of a professional social worker that they are able to undertake this complex activity.

Reflection in action shares many features of other reflective activity. It:

- builds on and develops critical thinking;

- requires a deep approach to learning;

- explores beneath the surface and so involves challenge, doubt, uncertainty and contradictions;

- uses experiences and feelings as resources to assist in developing an understanding of what is going on;

- thinks about things from different perspectives;

- is aided by understanding and self-awareness of how you grasp and deal with things.

However, it is more challenging than reflection on action because it requires all this while you are in the middle of an interaction, rather than in the luxurious position of being able to reflect after the event. So it requires clear, swift and multifaceted thinking while also being engaged in a conversation or discussion, often in difficult circumstances. The purpose of reflection in action is to be able to understand what is going on at different levels of the interaction, while also being a participant. It should enable a social worker to appreciate if, why and how their approach needs to change – and to be able to respond in a different way. Developing these skills can be helped by:

- building your reflective skills and self-awareness through reflection on action;

- good preparation for interactions, where possible, so you go about your work with a clear mind and open to the unexpected;

- a sound appreciation of theories of human relations such as transference, counter-transference, projection and defence mechanisms;

- flexibility in your style – being able to shift your approach in response to your developing understanding of events and processes.

RESEARCH SUMMARY

In Redmond's (2006) study, the students gave their thoughts on reflection in action (p121):

Watch it, realise what's happening and do something about it.

You have to stop yourself and think. You suddenly listen to what you are saying...you catch yourself...but once you can see what's happening you can be different.

CASE STUDY

Saranita's second placement

Saranita's second placement was in a children's centre. She was carrying out a piece of planned play work with a young mother, Ella, and her three-year-old son, Joe. The purpose was to enable Ella to extend Joe's learning through play. They had agreed to meet once a week for eight weeks. By the third week it had generally gone well. Saranita always planned carefully; she had read about children's development, the importance of play and activities. She knew Joe was interested in cars and devised play activities that would build on this. She appreciated Ella's anxiety about keeping her home clean and so tried to make suggestions that respected this so Ella could continue the play at home. Every week Saranita modelled a play activity and gradually handed over responsibility to Ella. At each session Ella took more responsibility and was building in confidence.

Saranita kept a reflective diary of the sessions. She had observed that sometimes she was enjoying playing with Joe so much that it was hard for her to hand over – though her self-awareness of this helped her to keep an appropriate focus. She had also reflected on Ella tending to want to hand back responsibility for Joe if he became distracted from the play. However, she was not prepared for what happened during the fifth session. The activity,

CASE STUDY *continued*

which Ella had taken over, was using dough which they had made from flour and water. Joe picked up a lump of the dough and threw it at his mother; it stuck in her hair. Ella's response was to grab Joe and scream and shout at him. He then burst into tears, Ella let go of him and he ran into a corner of the playroom. Ella then sat sobbing. It all happened very quickly. Saranita was not aware of any previous concern about Ella shouting at Joe.

A number of thoughts piled into Saranita's mind.

This is all my fault, what have I done wrong? She worked hard to discard these as not helpful to managing the situation and tried to reframe her thinking.

What had been going on? Why did Ella react in that way? It seemed like an over- reaction. What had Ella said to Joe?

What do I know that can help me with this?

Is Joe OK? Is Ella OK?

What do I need to do to help resolve the situation?

What shall I do? Should I call someone else?

Saranita was aware that the suddenness of the incident and the vehemence in Ella's tone had frightened her and she was shaken. Her own family was very gentle and she was not used to shouting. She took a deep breath to calm herself and help her think. She then recalled that Ella had said something like just the same as your dad you spiteful little bastard. *Saranita wondered about Joe's father and his behaviour to Ella. Was Ella transferring to Joe her feelings about his father?*

Saranita noticed that both Ella and Joe were quietly sobbing – neither approaching the other – almost as if they were used to this. Building on her previous knowledge of Ella, she gently approached her and suggested that together they went to Joe and that Ella could comfort him. Although Joe resisted initially, Ella was able to take him on her lap, calm him and spontaneously say sorry to him. Saranita sat with them quietly, aiming to give a message of support to both. Later Saranita was able to talk to Ella, recall what had happened and suggest that they should meet to discuss it some more – Ella agreed to this.

The incident took only a few minutes. It will have taken you longer to read and absorb the account of it than it did to occur. Yet within that time Saranita was able to use her, not perfect but good enough, skills of reflection in action to respond insightfully to a difficult situation that might have resulted in Ella not returning to the children's centre.

ACTIVITY 11.6

Using reflection in action

Think of an example from your own practice of using reflection in action. Evaluate your ability to do this.

152

C H A P T E R   S U M M A R Y

In this chapter we have explored the complexity and uncertainty of social work practice. Appreciating the context and building on the skills covered in earlier chapters, we have considered three approaches to support constructively working in this context. It should be apparent that taking an active and a deep approach to learning will be required for you to be able to grow and develop to this point. Using these approaches together should enable you to be a professional with reasoning, emotion and intelligence who can react reflectively, recognise many viewpoints and complexities, use a range of skills and knowledge creatively from diverse sources, create knowledge and transfer it to other contexts. This should assist you in making wise decisions in the uncertain conditions of social work practice. In the final chapter we will focus more on this synthesis, particularly considering the final project or undergraduate dissertation.

FURTHER READING

The following books deal in more depth with ethical dilemmas.

Banks, S (2006) *Ethics and values in social work*. 3rd edition. Basingstoke: Palgrave.

Watson, F et al. (2002) *Integrating theory and practice in social work education*. London: Jessica Kingsley (Chapter 6).

Smith, R (2005) *Values and practices in children's services*. Basingstoke: Palgrave.

Seden, J (2008) *Organisations and organisational change*. In Fraser, S and Matthews, S (eds) *The critical practitioner in social work and health care*. London: Sage, pp169–85.

A useful chapter on working within changing organisations

Taylor, C and White, S (2001) Knowledge, truth and reflexivity: The problem of judgement in social work, *Journal of Social Work*, 1 (37), 37–59.

This article provides some examples of different constructions of knowledge about social work.

Trevithick, P (2005) *Social work skills: A practice handbook*. Maidenhead: Open University Press / McGraw-Hill, pp272–4.

This provides a helpful summary of key concepts in psychosocial approaches (the unconscious, defence mechanisms, transference).

153

Chapter 12

Pulling it all together: Complexity, synthesis and the dissertation

A C H I E V I N G   A   S O C I A L   W O R K   D E G R E E

This chapter will help you to meet the following National Occupational Standards.
Key Role 6: Demonstrate professional competence in social work practice.
- Research, analyse, evaluate and use current knowledge of best social work practice.
- Work within agreed standards of social work practice and ensure own professional development.
- Manage complex ethical dilemmas and conflicts.

It will introduce you to the following academic standards set out in the social work subject benchmark statement.
5.5.1 Honours graduates in social work should be able to plan problem-solving activities, i.e. to
- think logically, systematically, critically and reflectively.

5.5.2 Honours graduates in social work should be able to
- gather information from a wide range of sources and by a variety of methods, for a range of purposes
- take into account differences of viewpoint in gathering information and critically assess the reliability and relevance of the information gathered.

5.5.3 Honours graduates in social work should be able to analyse and synthesise knowledge gathered for problem-solving purposes, i.e. to
- assess human situations, taking into account a variety of factors (including the views of participants, theoretical concepts, research evidence, legislation and organisational policies and procedures)
- analyse information gathered, weighing competing evidence and modifying their viewpoint in light of new information, then relate this information to a particular task, situation or problem
- assess the merits of contrasting theories, explanations, research, policies and procedures
- synthesise knowledge and sustain reasoned argument.

5.5.6 Honours graduates in social work should be able to
- write accurately and clearly in styles adapted to the audience and, purpose and context of the communication
- present conclusions verbally and on paper, in a structured form, appropriate to the audience for which these have been prepared.

5.5.8 Honours graduates in social work should be able to
- advance their own learning and understanding with a degree of independence
- take responsibility for their own further and continuing acquisition of knowledge and skills.

It will help you meet the Quality Assurance Agency for Higher Education (2001) requirement that students studying at Level 3 (H level) are able to demonstrate:
i. a systematic understanding of key aspects of their field of study, including acquisition of coherent and detailed knowledge, at least some of which is at, or informed by, the forefront of defined aspects of a discipline;

and

a. apply the methods and techniques that they have learned to review, consolidate, extend and apply their knowledge and understanding and to initiate and carry out projects;

b. critically evaluate arguments, assumptions, abstract concepts and data (that may be incomplete) to make judgements, and to frame appropriate questions to achieve a solution – or identify a range of solutions – to a problem;

c. communicate information, ideas, problems and solutions to both specialist and non-specialist audiences;

d. the ability to manage their own learning and to make use of scholarly reviews and primary sources, e.g. refereed research articles and/or original materials appropriate to the discipline.

Introduction

In this chapter we will consider what is required of social work students at the final stage of their studies. While courses differ, on many these academic skills will be tested through an extended piece of written work, project or dissertation. On the Diploma in Social Work, the social work qualification which preceded the degree, this was known as the integrated assignment. It shared many characteristics of the dissertation but obviously did not require Level H academic skills.

Within the constraints of course guidelines the dissertation can provide an opportunity for students to select their own topic, decide on their approach and work in a self-directed and independent way. It provides the opportunity for bringing together, using and extending learning on the course so far. Students who make the most of this chance find that their maturity as a learner is positively enhanced. This development equips them with skills and attributes which are directly transferable to employment and social work practice such as: the ability to work independently; time management; report writing; analysis and synthesis.

After reading this chapter you should know how to:

- appreciate what is required in a dissertation;

- use planning, organisational and thinking skills to complete a project;

- synthesise a range of perspectives and knowledges about a topic to develop new thinking.

The dissertation or project

The structure and organisation of social work programmes will vary. However, most require students to complete a dissertation, project or extended essay in the final stages of the course. This differs significantly from other assessed work in length, depth and complexity. On some courses students may be expected to carry out small-scale original research but this is not necessarily a requirement and will not be covered here. It is more likely that students will use research skills in searching for and analysing existing or secondary data. In the dissertation students have the opportunity to individually choose a topic of interest and, within the course assessment criteria, explore it in a way that fascinates them. It requires more prolonged, sustained and deeper engagement than with standard essays and assignments.

Very little has been written about undergraduate dissertations generally or on social work programmes. However, an exploration of course requirements suggests that, in order to successfully complete their dissertations or projects, students will need to:

- select their own topic and find an appropriate focus

- examine a relevant topic in depth

- systematically search and review literature

- select appropriate and relevant information

- explore different perspectives on the topic

- evaluate the material gathered

- think critically, analytically and reflectively

- manage the volume of material

- organise their thinking

- synthesise the range of perspectives and different knowledge on the topic

- make relevant connections with the practice of social work

- structure their work

- use tutorial support

- work independently and methodically

- present a cogently argued, clearly written, logically structured piece of work.

ACTIVITY 12.1

The challenges of the dissertation

Reflect on yourself as a learner. What specific challenges does the dissertation present for you?

Comment

Later in the chapter we will explore some of these issues in more depth. Here it is worth remembering that in order to successfully complete your dissertation you will need to utilise, build on and develop further all the aspects of studying we have already considered. These are:

- making connections between theory, knowledge and practice (Chapters 3 and 6)

- critical evaluation and analysis (Chapter 5)

- being a reflective learner and practitioner (Chapters 7 and 11)

- being research-informed (Chapter 9)

- being an independent, autonomous learner (Chapter 10)

- managing complexity (Chapter 11).

You may find it useful to revisit the chapters that are particularly relevant to the aspects of learning you find especially challenging.

Students' experiences

When thinking about working on your dissertation it may also be helpful to learn from other students who have successfully produced one.

RESEARCH SUMMARY

My experience of supervising students is consistent with the limited research on undergraduate dissertations and integrated assignments. Below are some significant comments from students about how they found the process.

- *The relative freedom to pursue your own topic was enjoyable.*

- *The sense of individual ownership of the work was motivating.*

- *Individual choice of the topic can lead to the study having real personal meaning.*

- *There was pleasure in mastering new ways of learning, seeing an issue from different perspectives, developing deeper understanding and managing the complexity of a big project.*

- *Working on the dissertation required high personal investment.*

- *It was very time consuming.*

- *The experience was emotionally unsettling. This was because students shifted between intellectual confusion and moments of insight and order.*

- *Producing the dissertation was not easy but was worthwhile.*

- *General support from other students could be helpful but, because dissertations are so individual, talking to other students could be counterproductive and produce panic.*

- *Working constructively with a supervisor was very important.*

- *The final part was the most demanding but also the most rewarding.*

- *The submission date seemed almost artificial, as if it would never come, and then suddenly it arrived.*

(Watson et al., 2002; Todd et al., 2004).

These observations highlight that the dissertation requires great commitment and, because it involves developing new thinking, is demanding but also rewarding. My experience suggests that part of the sense of achievement is in rising to the demands and overcoming the challenges. Next we will explore three important learning approaches which should help you in this: using supervision; organisation and planning; synthesis and problem-solving. While these aspects of working on a dissertation have been separated out so they are clear for you, in practice you will find that they are closely related and can complement each other; for example, you can use your organisational skills to find ways of developing clarity about different approaches and putting together an effective structure can be assisted by analytic and reflective thinking.

Using supervision

Most colleges will allocate an individual supervisor for this piece of work. This can position you in a new and different learning relationship with a tutor. Previously it is likely that your tutorials will have been conducted in groups – now you will be working in a one-to-one academic relationship, possibly for the first time. Because of the importance of the dissertation and because this is an individual piece of work, it is likely to be a more intense process. You will be asked to present your thoughts and ideas and to share your work in progress. It is possible that you will feel exposed by this and anxious about appearing foolish. In my experience students sometimes unhelpfully avoid tutorials because of this fear. It is important to be reflective about your feelings about this tutorial relationship in order that you are able use it as constructively as possible.

Your tutor will have different roles during your work on the dissertation: they may have subject expertise or they may be able to signpost you to other expert knowledge; they will support you in managing the project through timetabling and organisation of resources; they can provide guidance on structuring and writing; they will read drafts and give you feedback; they will act as a mentor to aid your reflection and critically analytic thinking; they may provide editorial direction on your writing.

It is important to clarify with your tutor the practical boundaries of the tutorial such as frequency, timing, cancellation, postponement and recording. You both need to be clear about your expectations of working together, for instance what email or telephone contact is agreed as acceptable between tutorials. It is useful to record all these issues in an agreement. At the beginning of the work on your dissertation you may find you need more support, as selecting a topic and finding an appropriate focus, together with planning targets for a piece of work of this size, are among the hardest aspects of the dissertation. As you proceed with the dissertation, learn how best to use feedback and become more confident, you should become a more autonomous learner and require less detailed guidance from your tutor (Todd et al., 2006).

ACTIVITY **12.2**

Using one-to-one tutorial support

Reflect on your feelings about one-to-one tutorial support. Identify the positives and negatives for you. Think about what you need to do to maximise the opportunity.

CASE STUDY

Nicola and her dissertation tutor

Nicola had submitted her dissertation topic as requested and been allocated Martin Jones as her tutor. He had taught the law and social work module and Nicola had found him a little daunting. Other students thought she was lucky as he was perceived to be knowledgeable and challenging. However, Nicola felt that under his scrutiny she would find it difficult to explain her ideas. Rather than arranging her first tutorial as was expected on the course timetable, she started working on her own. Over coffee Nicola's critical friend Mandy enthused about her first tutorial – how it had been challenging but given her focus. Nicola reluctantly shared with Mandy why she hadn't arranged to meet with Martin. Mandy helped her reflect on this and Nicola recalled experiences from school of feeling humiliated because she didn't get things right. Mandy encouraged her to get on with fixing a tutorial. Then Nicola bumped into Martin in the corridor and he suggested a time. At the first tutorial Nicola shared some of her anxieties with Martin. This was helpful in setting the context for their future work. Nicola also quickly realised that if she had arranged the tutorial earlier, her initial work on the dissertation could have been more productive.

Organisation and planning

Being able to handle the size and complexity of the work involved in your dissertation is one aspect of becoming an autonomous learner. While you will have support from a tutor, the overall responsibility for managing the various aspects of the dissertation lies with you. Developing habits of self-motivation and self-discipline will help you to focus on the aspects set out below.

Select your topic and focus

As discussed above, this is a difficult stage. However, it should not be delayed as time for working on your dissertation is at a premium. Remember that the dissertation is an opportunity to delve deeper and explore more about an aspect of social work that really gripped, puzzled or grabbed you.

When choosing your topic, thinking about the following questions can be helpful.

- Is it appropriate to social work?

- Does it engage you? Will it sustain your interest when your energy and enthusiasm are flagging?

- Is there sufficient, accessible and varied literature?

- Can you approach it analytically?

- Is it fit for assessment – will it enable you to meet the criteria required by the course?

- Is it too broad? It is normally better to aim for depth and quality rather than breadth. Students almost invariably begin with topics that are very much too wide.

Within the topic you will then need to clarify your focus. Sometimes this can be done by formulating a question, which should be clear and straightforward. It might be framed in the form of a social work dilemma. This focus will set the boundaries for your dissertation and should be clear, contained and manageable. Unless you choose a narrow focus you risk producing a dissertation that is descriptive and general – and will therefore not meet the academic requirements at this level.

CASE STUDY

Dan's dissertation

During Dan's second placement in the children looked after team he developed a strong interest in outcomes for looked-after children and proposed this as a topic for his dissertation. Dan had some familiarity with the literature from using research to think about the group he had worked with (Chapter 9). At his first meeting with his tutor Yvonne, she suggested that, while an important and interesting area, it was too broad. Yvonne helped Dan talk through some of his practice experiences on his placement, including his groupwork, and identified further relevant literature. By the end of the tutorial Dan's topic had narrowed to 'Educational outcomes for children looked after' and his focus the role of social workers in supporting children looked-after with education.

Setting and using a timetable

Effective time management is fundamental to thorough work on and successful completion of your dissertation. It is helpful to set out a clear timetable of work, with targets. Working backwards from the deadline, you should aim to complete all stages a week before the submission date. This makes allowance for the inevitable crises: not being able to access literature; the computer blowing up; family problems; illness; and, if you are also in employment, unexpected demands at work. Your timetable should link to the structure and can help you to work out what needs to be done first, the different stages of the dissertation and planning ahead. Allowing yourself time to revise early drafts and to read the dissertation as a whole can avoid unnecessary repetition and ensure connections are made between different sections.

If you are working on your dissertation full time you will find it different from a usual college week when private study is interspersed with classes. So you need to figure out how you can best work in this way; for instance, when it is most helpful for you to take breaks and how to use them constructively to re-energise yourself. Understanding which, for you, are the most productive times of the day and maximising these can be balanced with finding easier tasks to do when you are tired or less able to take on challenging tasks.

The literature search and reading

You will be expected to be aware of up-to-date literature, legislation and policies and guidance which may mean that journals and other electronic information are more relevant and helpful to you than textbooks. The pace of policy change, such as the reorganisation of government ministries, is now so rapid that many textbooks are out of date before they are printed.

Bearing in mind the note of caution about the use of websites in Chapter 1, electronic searches can be very helpful. Social Care Online is a good place to begin. Other useful databases are Applied Social Science Index and Abstracts (ASSIA), PsycInfo and International Encyclopaedia of the Social and Behavioural Sciences (IESBS). Beware of time-wasting searches – your tutor should be able to give you guidance on search terms for your topic to avoid fruitless activity. Always read the abstracts of journal articles with your topic in mind so that you can be clear about their potential usefulness.

Aim to read in a purposeful and focused way, bearing in mind the themes in your dissertation but without being too blinkered. As you read you should be alert to how different theories, aspects of research and knowledge, perspectives and values relate to the focus of your dissertation and to each other – how well do they explain the issue; do they build on each other; are they complementary or contradictory? Keep clear notes and use highlighter pens and sticky notes to mark significant points or passages.

Using organisational skills

One practical way of managing the complexity of the dissertation is to use good organisational skills. You need a system of keeping papers, books, notes and drafts where you can easily find them. When you start you will probably not foresee how much material you will generate. Write everything down – your thoughts, struggles, lists of resources you need and issues you need to pursue – a notebook can be useful for this. Ensure you keep a note of the references you are using systematically from the beginning. It is most frustrating to have to search for a piece of information such as the date of publication, when your time could be better used editing and improving your work. You will also need to have a means of organising your thoughts especially as the complexity of the topic develops and you explore different perspectives. Mind maps™ or colour coding can help to manage this material.

Finally, you need a good overall draft structure for the dissertation before you start writing. This usually necessitates identifying the main themes, each of which will be covered in a chapter. In addition, each chapter should be structured before you begin to write. Draft structures can always be revised in the light of new theories, research or insights. However, without this level of organisation you can easily lose focus and spend unproductive time. Having examples of dissertations written by students in previous years can assist you in appreciating how good organisation and structure can help you meet the requirements of your course.

CASE STUDY

Nicola's structure

Nicola chose to write her dissertation on 'Dilemmas in social work and hospital discharge'. Her tutor, Martin, helped her to organise the preliminary structure as follows.

Chapter One: Introduction

The topic and my focus; why I chose the topic.

CASE STUDY *continued*

My placement and some service users I worked with.

The practice dilemmas I experienced.

The structure and organisation of the dissertation.

Chapter 2: Working in an institution

The practice dilemmas of working in an institution. Theories and research which help to understand this, e.g. power; institutionalisation; the impact on older people of the loss they experience in hospital.

Chapter 3: Contradictions in policy and practice on ageism

What government policy (National Service Framework) says about ageism and what is the everyday experience of older people (drawing on research, service user experiences and observations from my placement). Relevant legislation: NHS and Community Care Act 1990; the Community Care (Delayed Discharge) Act 2003. Experiences of ageism highlighting gender and race issues.

Chapter 4: Working in a multidisciplinary team

An outline of the medical and the social models. An analysis of how the differences between them were played out in multidisciplinary teams in the hospital and in the experiences of older people.

Chapter 5: Positive practice

How, given all these dilemmas, social workers can practise positively. Findings from research. My practice and the approaches I used. Reflection on practice.

Chapter 6: Summary and conclusion

Having explored this issue in depth and complexity, what are my conclusions?

References and Bibliography.

ACTIVITY **12.3**

Developing a structure

Read in detail the assessment criteria for the dissertation, project or extended essay on your course. Then, with a topic in mind, put together a structure which will provide a framework within which you can organise your study.

Writing and editing

Aim to write clearly and concisely, remembering your audience. Go back through the feedback you have received from previous assignments to identify your strengths and weaknesses in writing and actively take steps to improve in the ways suggested. As you write, check your arguments are clear and logical from sentence to sentence, from paragraph to paragraph and from chapter to chapter. After you have completed your first draft, read through it for different purposes – for sense, for clarity of your arguments, for typographical errors, for correct punctuation and grammar and for appropriate referencing. This will mean reading it many times – but without this you may not be able to proofread with the thoroughness required. Ensure you have met the assessment criteria and word-length requirements for your course.

The skills outlined above are necessary for successful completion of your dissertation, but they are not sufficient. In the next section we will explore the academic skills needed.

Synthesis and identifying new thinking

In the previous chapter, we explored the complexity of social work practice and this included an appreciation of the contested nature of social work knowledge. Here we will focus again on managing complexity but with a specific focus on meeting the requirements of the dissertation. Complexity arises from the sheer number of sources of knowledge you might draw on; the range of types of knowledge, constructed in different ways, and the diverse perspectives that these will bring to you attention. Here we will focus on how you can approach dealing with these contributions to understanding a topic in social work and consider how they can be brought together or synthesised to enable new directions or approaches to understanding an issue.

To synthesise means to combine different elements into a coherent whole. For example, in music a synthesiser generates and combines signals of different frequencies to make new sounds. At Level H of your studies you are expected to be able to synthesise the different, and often competing, views on a topic; achieving this successfully can lead to identifying new ways of understanding or perceiving an issue and the implications for social work policy and practice. Next we consider some stages in this process of learning – achieving synthesis and identifying new directions. In order practically to manage the volume of material you will assemble for your dissertation, it can be helpful to follow these stages for each of the chapters.

Drawing on different sources of knowledge

The possible ways of understanding any topic in social work, and hence what you would need to include in your dissertation, might be drawn from:

- theories which aim to explain the issue
- social work values and ethics
- research studies
- social work practitioner knowledge and experience or practice wisdom
- knowledge from the experiences of different groups of service users
- knowledge from the experience of carers.

In each of these areas, particularly theories, research and values, you are likely to find more than you can possibly include in your dissertation. Hence you need to be selective, choosing those theories which you consider best throw light on the topic and research studies which are most helpful in developing understanding. You must be clear about your reasons for this selection and justify your decision within the dissertation. When making your selection it is important to think about the different levels at which social work can be understood: macro – the societal and structural level; mezzo – the organisational level of policy and procedures; and micro – the level of day-to-day practice. Aim to use theories and research concerned with each level. This enables you to take a holistic approach to the topic, showing that you grasp the significance of understanding the individual and day-to-day practice in a wider structural context of inequality and disadvantage.

Contested and competing knowledge

Of the theories and research you select, each can provide a lens for viewing the question or issue, presenting you with a new angle on the topic. Every perspective you include will impart a different understanding; telling a distinct story about a situation. You need to ensure you have a clear understanding of all the theories, research, values and perspectives you select, in order that you can work with them at a higher academic level. If you are struggling with a particular theory, you could discuss this with your tutor. You may find it helpful to refer back to Chapter 3, where some guidelines for grasping theory were set out, or to Chapter 8, in which we explored some ways of understanding research.

Evaluation, critical analysis and reflection

Once you have achieved clarity you should critically analyse, reflect on and evaluate each of the areas of knowledge and understanding on which you are drawing. Using evaluation and critical analysis, as explored in Chapters 4, 5 and 9 will enable you to identify:

- the strengths and weaknesses of the diverse theories, research, knowledge and perspectives you have selected;

- the relevance and contribution of each to understanding of the topic;

- the consistency of each with the values of social work.

Taking a reflective approach as outlined in Chapters 7 and 10 should ensure you understand why you might be more drawn to some theories and perspectives than others, and the implications of this for your analysis and evaluation.

Relating the ideas to each other

Consider the relative strengths and weaknesses of each your sources in relation to each other.
Considering sources of knowledge in relation to each other is a step towards managing the complexity of different understandings. For instance, you might find that accounts from service users are strong on conveying feelings and building a picture of what it is like

to need to be a recipient of services, but relatively weak on theorising explanations for services being organised in particular ways. In contrast, a research study might have identified ten different models for organising services but not the impact of each on the recipients of the service.

Consider the relative merits of the sources in relation to each other

Next consider the different sources of knowledge in relation to each other. This means asking whether they reinforce, support, contradict or challenge each other – or whether they are linked in other ways. Aim to appreciate their differences and commonalities. If you have carried out your reading in a focused way, alert to the need for this kind of analysis, you will find it easier to achieve the necessary clarity.

Hold these competing ideas simultaneously

Aim to hold, in your mind, simultaneously and in creative tension, the different perspectives without drawing conclusions or rushing to judgement. This is complex and may be assisted by using diagrams and coloured marker pens to graphically illustrate differences and connections.

Make connections and developments

Finally, make relevant connections, between the ideas you have generated, which throw light on the social work topic you have chosen. Develop arguments which incorporate and explain these ideas. In this way you should be able to build an integrated and cohesive account relating to the focus of your topic – answering the question or providing an explanation for the dilemma you originally posed. Aiming to put these ideas in writing clearly can alert you to aspects of your thinking which are not yet fully worked through. This may require you to retrace your steps and re-examine and rework your ideas.

Use this understanding to develop new thinking

Having explored the topic thoroughly and thrown new light on it, your insights should lead to new and innovative thinking. This might mean a different approach to practice; a changed understanding of an aspect of social work; possible resolution of a practice dilemma; a proposed different direction for policy. Sometimes students are so relieved to have completed the other parts of the dissertation that they do not give sufficient attention to this final part. It can be helpful to ensure this aspect of your dissertation is included in your structure from the beginning so you ensure it is not neglected or squeezed out.

ACTIVITY 12.4

Synthesising your material

Think about one chapter or theme within your dissertation and follow the steps above to achieve synthesis of your material and the development of new thinking.

CASE STUDY

Saranita's dissertation

Within the constraints of this book it is difficult to provide an in-depth, detailed and fully worked instance of synthesis and developing new thinking as required in a dissertation. However, the small-scale example presented below should provide illustration.

The dissertation title Saranita agreed with her tutor was 'How can parenting groups in children's centres ensure the inclusion of men?' The focus of one chapter was 'Men as fathers'. This is a summary of Saranita's notes and work in progress.

Drawing on different sources of knowledge

Below are the sources Saranita drew on, organised by theme, with a précis of their relevance.

Sociology of the family

Abbott, P et al. (2005) An introduction to sociology. *Abingdon: Routledge.*

Sociological perspectives on the family – in particular the gendered experiences of family life and the sexual division of domestic labour in the family. Research suggests that men do not share responsibility for tasks in the home and this includes caring for children.

Critical social policy commentary

Daniel, B et al. (2005) Why gender matters for Every Child Matters, British Journal of Social Work, *35 (8), 1343–55.*

A critical analysis of the lack of differentiation between fathers and mothers in Every Child Matters *(DfES, 2003) which uses the term 'parent' throughout. Argues that more research is needed on current patterns of fathering.*

Lewis, J (2002) Policy and behaviour in Britain. In Hobson, B (ed.) Making men into fathers. *Cambridge: Cambridge University Press.*

Notes the negative assumption that underlies policy – that fathers are in flight from their financial obligations to maintain families.

Scourfield, J and Drakeford, M (2002) New Labour and the 'problem of men'. Critical Social Policy, *22 (4), 619–40.*

Observes that New Labour was generally positive about men as fathers although the commitment to initiatives supporting this varied across departments. Notes that wife-beaters and sex offenders are constructed in policy as 'non-fathers'.

Social work research with a psychological emphasis

Flouri, E and Buchanan, A (2003) The role of father involvement and mother involvement in adolescents' psychological well-being. British Journal of Social Work, *33 (3), 399–406.*

A study concluding that father involvement had a strong relationship with adolescents' psychological well-being.

Social workers' views of men as parents

Scourfield, J (2006) The challenge of engaging fathers in the child protection process, Critical Social Policy, *26 (2), 440–9.*

Draws on ethnographic research in a social services office; notes that social workers tended to hold views of fathers as a threat, as no use and irrelevant.

Men's views

Speak, S et al., (1997) Young single fathers. *London: Family Policy Centre.*

Small-scale research study of 40 young, single, lone parent, non-residential fathers, exploring their perceptions and aspirations regarding their role as fathers. Concluded that the men felt strongly about their children and wanted to be good fathers but other role expectations, such as the need to be in employment, could be an obstacle.

Tyrer, P et al. (2005) 'Dealing with it': Experiences of young fathers in and leaving care, British Journal of Social Work, *35 (7), 1107–21.*

A more recent small study of 16 young fathers, who were, or had been, looked-after. It found that they expressed positive feelings towards their children but had found it difficult to establish their role. Economic and social barriers combined with the disadvantage associated with being looked-after.

Lupton, D and Barclay, L (1997) Constructing fatherhood; discourses and experiences. *London: Sage.*

Small-scale survey of fathers in the early stages of first-time parenting which found that men wanted to, and did, participate more actively in domestic labour and childcare. However, the demands of employment were an obstacle to this.

Fathers in the children's centre

Ghate, D et al. (2000) Fathers and family centres: engaging fathers in preventive services. *York: Joseph Rowntree Foundation.*

This small-scale research explored explanations for fathers' relative lack of involvement in family centres from the multiple perspectives of men using centres, men not using centres whose partners were, the wives and partners of the men and staff and managers in family centres. It concluded that family centres tend to be seen as 'women's places' or as 'women and children's places' and the reasons for this were the way in which centres were managed, staffed and organised – while mothers were welcomed as women in their own right, men were not. Fathers who wanted to engage with all the centre activities could only do so on women's terms.

I also carried out a very small-scale study of the four fathers who attended the parenting groups at the children's centre – they expressed strong views about the importance of men taking an equal role in the family.

The views of the children's centre staff

In a staff meeting discussion about my dissertation, colleagues gave their views. There was almost total agreement that men talked a lot about wanting to be good parents but had a tendency to opt for the more fun parts. Unlike women, they had more opportunity to opt out of the less pleasant aspects of parenting. The staff also raised the dilemmas for them when working with fathers who had been violent towards children's mothers.

Children's views

Featherstone, B (2003) Taking fathers seriously, British Journal of Social Work, 33 (2), 239–54.

A range of views is presented. Of particular interest was a study which asked children what they wanted from fathers – the five areas were a role model, quality time, supportive behaviour, expression of love, physical contact.

Mullender, A et al. (2002) Children's perspectives on domestic violence. London Sage.

Because of the views of the children's centre staff it seemed worthwhile to read about the views of children in families where the father had been violent to their mother. The very mixed emotions these children expressed were fear, sadness, love, hatred and bewilderment.

Evaluation, critical analysis and reflection

These are the some of the points I considered.

- *Some studies are very small-scale; how representative are they?*

- *The category 'father' is used as if it is universally applicable and this obscures differences – class, socioeconomic status, race, age, sexual orientation, culture. There is a risk of generalising from limited studies to all fathers.*

- *Some research is not very current – have the roles of men changed significantly in the last decade?*

- *Is there an inconsistency between some of the experiences of fathers and the views expressed by professionals and the social work value of respect for individuals? How can this be resolved?*

I reflected on how my own experience of being raised in a single-parent Muslim family might impact on the way I think about men as fathers. My dad died when I was three years old – so reading about positive fathering leaves me feeling sad. But I think I experienced a different kind of fathering because the Muslim community was a strong source of support to my mother and to me. At times I felt a little uncomfortable with some of the views expressed by children's centre staff.

Relating the ideas to each other

No clear picture has emerged from my reading so far – there are many competing views. While research studies seem to suggest that men wish to become more engaged in

CASE STUDY *continued*

fathering, it is not really clear what this means. Overall it seems to suggest being more involved with their children but this does not seem to be universally achieved. Traditional views of the man as breadwinner still pertain and this is an obstacle to involved father-hood. Policy initiatives are not generally helpful – among the difficulties are long working hours for men and lower pay for women. Children seem to have a clear view of what they hope for from fathers but the impact of domestic violence complicates the issue. This was also the case when looking at perspectives of staff in children's centres.

New thinking

I would argue that the category 'father' has limited usefulness and needs to be differentiated further in relation to other aspects of identity. Does the category 'father who is violent to the mother of his children' need to be acknowledged and explored more?

More creative approaches to father- and mother-friendly *social policies could be helpful.*

Fatherhood may be problematic in children's centres, which tend to be female-focused environments – most staff and adult users are women and the impact of domestic violence is a live issue. But this raises questions about inclusiveness.

There is a lack of consensus about what a father should be – so what criteria are social workers using when they carry out assessments? What has been the role of the Framework for Assessment of Children in Need and their Families (Department of Health, 2000) in this? It would be useful to explore in more depth social work values and how professionals work with fathers.

Conclusion

In this chapter we have explored the dissertation, which will for many be the final, and most demanding, piece of work during your degree. While it has not been possible to consider every aspect in detail, the focus here will hopefully have been helpful to understanding the purpose and requirements of a dissertation and helpful ways of going about such a project. Ultimately most students seem to appreciate having the opportunity to challenge themselves and to have produced such an individual piece of work. I hope you do too.

FURTHER READING

Cottrell, S (2003) *The study skills handbook*. 2nd edition. Basingstoke: Palgrave.
This book includes a dissertation checklist and action plan which may be useful in helping you with organisation.

Watson, F et al. (2002) *Integrating theory and practice in social work education*. London: Jessica Kingsley.
This was written to support students in writing the integrated assignment for the Diploma in Social Work but nevertheless includes some useful suggestions.

There are several websites which provide advice on dissertations; they may be helpful, but remember you will be writing an undergraduate dissertation for a degree in social work – hence advice on dissertations for higher-level degrees and generic guidance may not be helpful. It is more important that you give careful attention to the requirements of your own course.

Conclusion

Studying for a degree in social work can be exciting, rewarding and challenging. Sometimes the difficulties that students face can overwhelm and obscure the stimulation and thrill of learning. This book arose from my observations that students need support and guidance with developing specific academic skills within the context of studying for social work. Without this it can be difficult for students to make progress and maximise their opportunities for personal and professional development. If the book has been a support to you during your degree studies and helped you to better appreciate effective academic study then it will have achieved its aim.

Having reached this part of the book you will be nearing the end of your social work degree. Depending on your mode of study this might have taken you three or four years and you will be close to qualifying as a social worker. During this time you will have been through many significant learning experiences, both while in college and on placement. When you reflect back on this period of your life you will no doubt recall good times and hard times, highs and lows, frustration and joy, pleasure and pain. Take the time to consider how you have changed during your course both personally and professionally. You might find it particularly useful to identify how you have developed as a learner. This understanding will be valuable as you begin practising as a social worker and begin a new phase of learning. One theme of the book has been the complexity of social work practice and hence the need for practitioners to incorporate different perspectives and think clearly, analytically and reflectively. These skills should equip you to continue to grow and develop in your social work career. I wish you well as you enter the profession of social work.

References

Abbott, P, Wallace, C and Tyler, M (2005) *An Introduction to sociology: Feminist perspectives*. Abingdon: Routledge.

Adams, R (2003) *Social work and empowerment.* Basingstoke: BASW Macmillan.

Adams, R et al. (eds) (1998) *Social work: Themes, issues and critical debates.* Basingstoke: Macmillan.

Aldgate J and Jones, D (2006) The place of attachment in children's development. In Aldgate, J et al. (eds) *The developing world of the child.* London: Jessica Kingsley.

Alston, M and Bowles, W (2003) *Research for social workers. An introduction to methods.* 2nd edition. Abingdon: Routledge.

Banks, S (2006) *Ethics and values in social work.* Basingstoke: Palgrave.

Barn, R, Andrew, L and Mantovani, N (2005) *Life after care. The experiences of young people from different ethnic groups.* York: Joseph Rowntree Foundation.

Barnes, C, Oliver, M and Barton, L (2002) Introduction. In Barnes, C, Oliver, M and Barton, L (eds) *Disability studies today.* Oxford: Blackwell.

Barnett, R (1994) *The limits of competence: Knowledge, higher education and society.* Buckingham: Open University Press.

Becker, S and Bryman, A (eds) (2004) *Understanding research for social policy and practice.* Bristol: Policy Press.

Beckett, C (2002) *Human growth and development.* London: Sage.

Beckett, C (2006) *Essential theory for social work practice.* London: Sage.

Beckett, C and Maynard, A (2005) *Values and ethics in social work.* London: Sage.

Bell, M and Wilson, K (2006) Children's views of family group conferences, *British Journal of Social Work*, 36 (4), 671–81.

Beresford, P (2001) Service users, social policy and the future of welfare, *Critical Social Policy,* 31 (4), 495–512.

Beresford, P and Evans, C (1999) Research note: Research and empowerment, *British Journal of Social Work,* 29 (5), 671–7.

Beresford, P and Croft, S. (2001) Service users' knowledges and the social construction of social work, *Journal of Social Work,* 1 (3), 295–316.

Biggs, J (2003) *Teaching for quality learning at university.* Maidenhead: Open University Press / McGraw-Hill.

Boud, D and Solomon, N (eds) (2001) *Work-based learning: A new higher education?* Maidenhead: Open University Press / McGraw-Hill.

Boud, D, Keogh, R and Walker, D (1985) *Reflection: Turning experience into learning.* London: Kogan Page.

Brown, A (2002) Groupwork. In Davies, M (ed.) *The companion to social work.* Oxford: Blackwell.

Burke, D (2007) How students use feedback. Association for Learning and Development in Higher Education Symposium 12.4.2007 **www.lincol.ac.uk/ldhen/jiscmail.htm**

Butler, I and Drakeford, M (2001) Which Blair project? Communitarianism, social authoritarianism and social work, *Journal of Social Work,* 1(1), 7–19.

Butt, J and O'Neil, A (2004) *'Lets move on'. Black and Minority Ethnic older people's views on research findings.* York: Joseph Rowntree Foundation.

Carr, W (1995) *For education: Towards intial inquiry.* Buckingham: Open University Press.

Chan, V (2001) Readiness for learner autonomy: what do our learners tell us? In *Teaching in Higher Education,* 6 (4), 505–18.

Charles, M and Butler, S (2004) Social workers' management of organisational change. In Lymbery and Butler (2004).

Cheetham, J (2002) The research perspective. In Davies, M. (ed.) *Companion to Social Work.* Oxford: Blackwell.

Chima, G (2003) The juggling act. In Cree V (2003).

Clare, B (2007) Promoting deep learning: A teaching, learning and assessment endeavour, *Social Work Education,* 26 (5), 433–46.

Clarke, J and Newman, J (1997) *The managerial state.* London: Sage.

Cohen, S (1973) *Folk devils and moral panics. The creation of mods and rockers.* London: Paladin.

Coleman, H, Rogers, G and King, J (2002) Using portfolios to stimulate critical thinking in social work education, *Social Work Education,* 21 (5), 583–95.

Cooper, B (2008) Continuing professional development. In Fraser, S and Matthews, S (2008).

Corby, B (2006) *Applying research in social work practice.* Maidenhead: Open University Press / McGraw-Hill.

Cottrell, S (2003) *The study skills handbook.* Basingstoke: Palgrave Macmillan.

Cottrell, S (2005) *Critical thinking skills.* Basingstoke: Palgrave Macmillan.

Coulshed, V and Orme, J (2006) *Social work practice.* Basingstoke: Palgrave.

Cree, V (2000) *Sociology for social workers and probation officers.* Abingdon: Routledge.

Cree, V (ed.) (2003) *Becoming a social worker.* Abingdon: Routledge.

Cree, V and Davis, A (2007) *Social work: Voices from the inside.* Abingdon: Routledge.

Cree, V and Macauley, C (eds) (2000) *Transfer of learning in professional and vocational education.* Abingdon: Routledge.

Davies, M (ed.) (2002) *Companion to social work.* Oxford: Blackwell.

Dempsey, M, Halton, C and Murphy, M (2001) Reflecting learning in social work education: scaffolding the process, *Social Work Education,* 20 (6), 631–41.

DfES (2006a) *Every Child Matters: report of consultation meetings with children and young people.* **www.dfes/everychildmatters.gov.uk**

DfES (2006b) *Working together to safeguard children.* London: The Stationery Office.

DfES (2006c) *Care Matters: Transforming the lives of children and young people in care.* London: The Stationery Office.

DfES (2007) *Care Matters*: *Time for change.* London: The Stationery Office.

Department of Health (2000) *Framework for the assessment of children in need and their families.* London: The Stationery Office.

Department of Heath (2001a) *National service framework for older people.* London: The Stationery Office.

Department of Health (2001b) *Studies informing the framework for the assessment of children in need and their families.* London: The Stationery Office.

Department of Health (2001c) *Valuing people.* London: The Stationery Office.

Department of Health (2002) *Requirements for social work training*. London: Department of Health.

Doel, M (2000) Practice teaching and learning. In Pierce, R and Weinstein, J *Innovative education and training for care professionals.* London: Jessica Kingsley.

Doel, M (2006) *Using groupwork.* Abingdon: Routledge.

Dominelli, L (1997) *Sociology for social work.* Basingstoke: Macmillan.

Dominelli, L (2004) *Social work.* Cambridge: Polity Press.

Dugmore, P and Pickford, J (2006) *Youth justice and social work.* Exeter: Learning Matters.

Dustin, D (2006) Skills and knowledge needed to practise as a care manager, *Journal of Social Work,* 6 (3), 293–313.

Edwards, R (1993) *Mature women students. Separating or connecting family and education.* Abingdon: Routledge.

Entwistle, N, McCune, V and Walker, P (2001) Conceptions, styles and approaches within higher education: Analytical abstractions and every-day experiences. In Sternberg and Zhang (eds) (2001) *Perspectives on thinking, learning and cognitive styles.* London: Lawrence Erlbaum Associates.

Eraut, M (1994) *Developing professional knowledge and competence.* Abingdon: Falmer Press.

Fawcett, B, Featherstone, B and Goddard, G (2004) *Contemporary child care policy and practice.* Basingstoke: Palgrave.

Fisher, T and Somerton, J (2000) Reflection on action: the process of helping social work students to develop their use of theory in practice, *Social Work Education,* 19 (4), 387–401.

Fook, J (2007) Theorizing from practice: Towards an inclusive approach for social work research, *Qualitative Social Work,* 1 (79), 79–95.

Ford, P et al. (2005) Practice learning and the development of students as critical practitioners – Some findings from research, *Social Work Education* 24(4), 391–407.

Fraser, S and Matthews, S (eds) (2008) *The critical practitioner in social work and health care.* London: Sage.

Freire, P (1972) *Pedagogy of the oppressed.* London: Penguin.

Garrett, PM (2003) *Remaking social work with children and families.* Abingdon: Routledge.

General Social Care Council (2002) *Codes of practice for social care workers and employers.* London: GSCC.

Ghate, D and Hazel, N (2003) *Parenting in poor environments.* London: Jessica Kingsley.

Gibbs, G (1981) *Teaching students to learn.* Buckingham: Open University Press.

Gibbons, J and Gray, M (2002) An integrated and experience-based approach to social work education: the Newcastle model, *Social Work Education,* 21 (5), 529–49.

Godel, M (2007) *Get the picture: older people's lives in rural West Oxfordshire 2004-2007.* Oxford: Age Concern.

Goffman, E (1961) *Asylums.* New York: Doubleday.

Gordon, D, Levitas, R and Pantazis, C (2006) *Poverty and social exclusion in Britain: The millenium survey.* Bristol: Policy Press.

Gould, N and Taylor, N (eds) (1996) *Reflective learning for social work.* Aldershot: Arena.

Graham, M (2007) *Black issues in social work and social care.* Bristol: Policy Press.

Gregory, M and Holloway, M (2005) Language and the shaping of social work, *British Journal of Social Work,* 35 (1), 37–53.

Harding, T and Beresford, P (1996*) The standards we expect: What service users and carers want from social services workers.* London: National Institute for Social Work.

Harrison, K and Ruch, G (2007) Social work and the use of self. On becoming and being a social worker. In Lymbery, M and Postle, K (2007).

Hawkins, L, Fook, J and Ryan, M (2001) Social workers' use of the language of social justice, *British Journal of Social Work,* 31(1), 1–13.

Healey, K (2005) *Social work theories in context.* Basingstoke: Palgrave Macmillan.

Hopkins, G (1998a) *Plain English for social services: A guide to better communication.* Lyme Regis: Russell House Publishing.

Hopkins, G (1998b) *The write stuff: A guide to effective writing in social care and related services.* Lyme Regis: Russell House Publishing.

Hopkins, G (2004) That Friday feeling, *Community Care,* 24–30 June, 40–1.

Horwath, J (ed.) (2001) *The child's world: Assessing children in need.* London: Jessica Kingsley.

Howe, D (1995) *Attachment theory for social work practice.* Basingstoke: Palgrave.

Howe, D (2001) Attachment. In Horwath, J (ed.) (2001) *The child's world: Assessing Children in Need.*

Howe, D (2002) Relating practice to theory. In Davies (2002).

Howe, D (2005) *Child abuse and neglect.* Basingstoke: Palgrave Macmillan.

Humphries, B (2007) Research mindedness. In Lymbery, M and Postle, K (2007).

Ingleby, E (2006) *Applied psychology for social work.* Exeter: Learning Matters.

Jackson, N (2004) Developing the concept of metalearning, *Innovations in Education and Teaching International,* 41 (4), 391–403.

Jackson, S et al. (2005) *Going to university from care.* London: Institute of Education.

Jones, C (2001) State social work and new labour. *British Journal of Social Work,* 31(4), 547–62.

Knott, C and Scragg, T (eds) (2007) *Reflective practice in social work.* Exeter: Learning Matters.

Koprowska, J (2005) *Communication and interpersonal skills in social work.* Exeter: Learning Matters.

Laming, Lord H (2003) *The Victoria Climbié inquiry report. CM 5730.* London: Stationery Office. Crown copyright. **www.victoria-climbie-inquiry.org.uk/fine/report.pdf**

Lishman, J (1998) Personal and professional development. In Adams, R et al. (1998).

Lishman, J (ed.) (2007) *Handbook for practice learning in social work and social care.* London: Jessica Kingsley.

Lister, PG (2000) Mature students and transfer of learning. In Cree, V and Macauley, C (2000).

Littlechurch, R and Glasby, J (2000) Older people as 'participating patients'. In Kemshall, H and Littlechild, R (eds) *User involvement and participation in social care.* London: Jessica Kingsley.

Lymbery, M and Butler, S (eds) (2004) *Social work ideals and practice realities.* Basingstoke: Palgrave.

Lymbery, M and Postle, K (2007) *Social work: A companion to learning.* London: Sage.

Lyons, F and Bennett, M (2001) Setting the standards: Judging levels of achievement. In Boud, D and Solomon, N (eds) *Work-based learning. A new higher education?* Buckingham: Open University Press.

Lyons, K (2002) Researching social work: doctoral work in the UK. *Social Work Education,* 21 (3), 337–46.

Macaulay, C (2000) Transfer of learning. In Cree, V and Macaulay, C (2000).

Marsh, P (2007) Task-centred practice. In Lishman (2007).

Marsh, P and Doel, M (2005) *The task-centred book.* Abingdon: Routledge.

Martin, P and Jackson, Y (2002) Educational success for children in public care: advice from a group of high achievers, *Child and Family Social Work,* 7 (2), 121–30.

McDonald, G and Turner, W (2005) An experiment in helping fostercarers manage challenging behaviour, *British Journal of Social Work,* 35 (8), 1265–82.

McLaughlin, H (2007) *Understanding social work research.* London: Sage.

Merton, J (2003) Social work in transition In Cree (2003).

Mezirow, J (1981) A critical theory of adult learning and education, *Adult Education,* 32 (1) 3–24.

Moon, J (2004) *A handbook of reflective and experiential learning.* Abingdon: Routledge.

Moon, J (2005) *We seek it here…a new perspective on the elusive activity of critical thinking; a theoretical and practical approach.* Bristol: ESCalate.

Mullender, A and Ward, D (1991) *Self-directed groupwork: Users take action for empowerment.* London: Whiting and Birch.

Nicolson, P, Bayne, R and Owen, J (2006) *Applied psychology for social workers.* Basingstoke: Palgrave Macmillan.

Northedge, A (2005) *The good study guide.* Buckingham: Open University Press.

Oliver, M and Sapey, B (2006) *Social work with disabled people.* Basingstoke: Macmillan.

Parker, J (2004) *Effective practice learning in social work.* Exeter: Learning Matters.

Parker, J and Bradley, G (2007) *Social work practice: Assessment, planning, intervention and review.* Exeter: Learning Matters.

Parton, N (1985) *The politics of child abuse.* Basingstoke: Macmillan.

Parton, N (2000) Some thoughts on the relationship between theory and practice in and for social work, *British Journal of Social Work,* 30 (4), 449–63.

Parton, N (2003) Rethinking professional practice: The contributions of social constructionism and the feminist 'ethics of care', *British Journal of Social Work,* 33 (1), 1–16.

Pawson, R, Boaz, A, Grayson, L, Long, A and Barnes, C (2003) *Types and quality of knowledge in social care: Knowledge review 3.* Bristol: SCIE/Policy Press.

Payne, G and Payne, J (2004) *Key concepts in social research.* London: Sage.

Payne, M (2005a) *Modern social work theory.* 3rd edition. Basingstoke: Palgrave Macmillan.

Payne, M (2005b) *The origins of social work: Continuity and change.* Basingstoke: Palgrave Macmillan.

Payne, M (2006) *What is professional social work?* Bristol: BASW/Policy Press.

Pierson, J (2002) *Tackling social exclusion.* Abingdon: Routledge.

Preston-Shoot, M (2007) *Effective groupwork.* Basingstoke: Macmillan.

Pugh, G (1999) *Unlocking the past: The impact of access to Barnardo's childcare records.* Aldershot: Ashgate.

Pugh, R (2007) Variations in registrations on child protection registers, *British Journal of Social Work,* 37 (1), 5–21.

Quality Assurance Agency for Higher Education (2001) *The framework for higher education qualifications in England, Wales and Northern Ireland.* (**www.qaa.ac.uk**)

Quality Assurance Agency for Higher Education (2008) *Subject benchmark statement for social work.* (**www.qaa.ac.uk**)

Rai, L (2006) Owning (up to) reflective writing in social work education, *Social Work Education,* 25 (6), 785–97.

Redmond, B (2006) *Reflection in action.* Aldershot: Ashgate.

Robinson, L (1995) *Psychology for social workers.* Abingdon: Routledge.

Rose, W (2006) The developing world of the child: Children's perspectives. In Aldgate, J, Jones, D, Rose, W and Jeffery, C (eds) *The developing world of the child.* London: Jessica Kingsley.

Rowlings, C (2000) Social work education and higher education: Mind the gap. In Pierce, R and Weinstein, J *Innovative Education and Training for Care Professionals.* London: Jessica Kingsley.

Ruch, G (2002) From triangle to spiral: reflective practice in social work education, practice and research, *Social Work Education,* 21 (2), 199–216.

Schön, DA (1983) *The reflective practitioner. How professionals think in action.* New York: Basic Books.

Secker, J (1993) *From theory to practice in social work.* Aldershot: Avebury.

Seden, J (2008) Organisations and organisational change. In Fraser and Matthews (2008).

Shardlow, S (2007) The social policy context of practice learning. In Lishman (2007).

Shaw, I and Gould, N (eds) (2001) *Qualitative research in social work.* London: Sage.

Shaw, I and Norton, M (2007) *The kinds and quality of social work research in UK universities.* London: SCIE.

Sheldon, B and McDonald, G (1999) *Research and practice in social care: Mind the gap.* Exeter: Centre for Evidence-Based Social Services.

Smith, R (2005) *Values and practices in children's services.* Basingstoke: Palgrave.

Sibeon, R (1990) Comments on the structure and forms of social work knowledge, *Social Work and Social Sciences Rev* 1 (1).

Social Exclusion Unit (2003) *A better education for children in care.* London: Office of the Deputy Prime Minister.

Statham, J (2007) The effect of family poverty on children, *Community Care,* 29 November, 24–5.

Stephenson, J (2001) Ensuring a holistic approach to work-based learning. In Boud and Solomon (2001).

Sternberg, RJ and Zhang, L (eds) (2001) *Perspectives on thinking, learning and cognitive styles.* London: Lawrence Erlbaum Associates.

SWAP (2007) *The social work degree; preparing to succeed.* (**www.swap.ac.uk**)

Taylor, C and White, S (2000) *Practising reflexivity in health and welfare.* Buckingham: Open University Press.

Taylor, C and White, S (2001) Knowledge, truth and reflexivity: The problem of judgement in social work. *Journal of Social Work,* 1 (37), 37–59.

Taylor, C and White, S (2006) Knowledge and reasoning in social work: Educating for humane judgement. *British Journal of Social Work,* 36 (6), 937–54.

Tew, J et al. (2006) *Values and methodologies for social research in mental health.* London: SCIE.

Thoburn, J, Chand, A and Proctor, J (2005) *Child welfare services for minority ethnic children.* London: Jessica Kingsley.

Thompson, N (2000) *Theory and practice in human services.* Maidenhead: Open University Press / McGraw-Hill.

Thompson, N (2006) *Anti-discriminatory practice.* Basingstoke: Palgrave Macmillan.

Thorpe, M (2000) Encouraging students to reflect as part of the assignment process, *Active Learning in Higher Education,* 1, (1), 79–92.

Todd, MJ et al. (2004) Independent inquiry and the undergraduate dissertation: perceptions and experiences of final-year social science students. *Assessment and Evaluation in Higher Education,* 29 (3), 335–55.

Todd, MJ et al. (2006) Supervising a social science undergraduate dissertation: staff experiences and perceptions. *Teaching in Higher Education,* 11 (2), 161–73.

TOPSS (2002a) *The National Occupational Standards for Social Work.* (**www.skillsforcare.org.uk**)

TOPSS (2002b) *Statement of expectations from individuals, families, carers, groups and communities who use services and those who care for them.* (**www.skillsforcare.org.uk**)

Trevillion, S (2000) Social work, social networks and network knowledge. *British Journal of Social Work,* 30(4), 505–17.

Trevithick, P (2005a) *Social work skills: a practice handbook.* Maidenhead: Open University Press / McGraw-Hill.

Trevithick, P (2005b) The knowledge base of groupwork and its importance within social work. *Groupwork,* 15 (2), 80–107.

Trinder, L (1996) Social work research: the state of the art (or science). *Child and Family Social Work,* 1(14), 233–42.

Twigg, J (2000) *Bathing – the body and community care.* Abingdon: Routledge.

VCC (2004a) *Start with the child, stay with the child.* London: Voice for the Child in Care.

VCC (2004b) *The care experience: Through black eyes.* London: Voice for the Child in Care.

Walker, S and Becket, C (2003) *Social work assessment and intervention.* Lyme Regis: Russell House.

Warren, J (2007) *Service user and carer participation in social work.* Exeter: Learning Matters.

Watson, F et al. (2002) *Integrating theory and practice in social work education.* London: Jessica Kingsley.

Weinstein, J (2008) *Working with loss, death and bereavement. A guide for social workers.* London: Sage.

White, V and Harris, J (2007) Management. In Lymbery, M and Postle, K (eds) *Social work: A companion to learning.* London: Sage.

Williams, F (1989) *Social policy: a critical introduction.* Cambridge: Polity Press.

Williams, P (2006) *Social work with people with learning difficulties.* Exeter: Learning Matters.

Index